C0-AWA-390

Berry-Hill

Francis A. Silva (1835–1886)

In His Own Light

Mark D. Mitchell

With an Introduction by John Wilmerding

BERRY-HILL GALLERIES, INC.

11 East 70th St., New York, NY 10021 212.744.2300

Contents

Acknowledgments

Rarely does an art gallery have the opportunity to present for the very first time the work of an art-historically important artist. Such is the case with this retrospective of Francis A. Silva, the distinguished but heretofore neglected Luminist. We are indebted to John Wilmerding (Sarofim Professor of American Art, Princeton University) for inspiring and supporting this exhibition and publication, which features his eloquent introduction and the fruits of Mark D. Mitchell's comprehensive research. Mr. Mitchell, who is completing his Ph.D. in 19th-century American Art under Professor Wilmerding, has produced the first in-depth biographical study of Silva as well as a catalogue of known works, which hopefully will be of scholarly use for many years to come. Most importantly, we would like to thank the generous lenders, listed separately, and our devoted associates, Daisy Hill Shea and David Hill, for conceiving and coordinating this project, and our dedicated staff, including Minora Collins for her diligent coordination of the loans, Vicki Marcantel for her management of this publication, Chris Ream for his beautiful installation, and Bruce Weber, Director of Exhibitions. In addition we are grateful to the following

collectors, scholars and institutions who have in various ways so graciously cooperated: Dr. Robert Aaronson; Dennis Anderson, Curator, New York State Capitol; Avery Galleries; Lillian Brenwasser, Kennedy Galleries; Mark Brock; Elizabeth Burns, Sotheby's Images; Teresa Carbone, Associate Curator of American Painting and Sculpture, Brooklyn Museum of Art; Mary Lineberger, Reproductions Coordinator, The Cleveland Museum of Art; Deanna Cross, Director of the Photograph Library, The Metropolitan Museum of Art; Courtney DeAngelis, Associate Registrar, Amon Carter Museum; Dan Finamore, Curator, Peabody Essex Museum; Jack Garrity; Nancy Hall-Duncan, Curator, The Bruce Museum of Arts and Science; Christine Hennessey, Research Administrator, Smithsonian American Art Museum; Jennifer Jensen, Assistant Registrar, New-York Historical Society; Kennedy Galleries; Tielle Larson, Rights and Reproduction, Santa Barbara Museum of Art; Maggie Mazzullo, Registrar, Munson Williams Proctor Arts Institute, Museum of Art; Museum of Fine Arts, Boston; Elizabeth Moodey, Doctoral Candidate, Department of Art & Archaeology, Princeton University;

Gillian Nagler, Assistant Curator, The Currier Gallery of Art; Richard Norton Gallery; Barbara Novak; Paul Provost, Senior Vice President and International Business Director, Christie's; Jenny Park, Marketing Coordinator, Christie's; George Schwartz, Curatorial Assistant, Maritime Department, Peabody Essex Museum; Paul D. Schweizer, Director and Chief Curator, Munson Williams Proctor Arts Institute, Museum of Art; Andrew Spahr, Curator, The Currier Gallery of Art; Theodore E. Stebbins; Judy Throm, Head of Reference, Archives of American Art, Smithsonian Institution; Vallejo Gallery; Kristen Weiss, Collections Manager, American Decorative Arts Department, Peabody Essex Museum; Edward T. Wilson; Richard York Gallery; and the staffs of the Archives of American Art, Smithsonian Institution, Washington; the Frick Art Reference Library; the New-York Historical Society Library; the New York Public Library Art Division; and the Peabody Essex Museum and Library. Mark Mitchell would like to dedicate his contributions to this exhibition to Rebecca Whitin with affection and gratitude.

Frederick D. Hill
James Berry Hill

Lenders to the Exhibition

Anonymous Lenders
The Bostonian Society
Brooklyn Museum of Art
The Bruce Museum of Arts and Science
Charles Butt
Maryann and Alvin Friedman
Howard and Melinda Godel
Lawrence and Jennifer Goichman
Elizabeth and Melville T. Hodder
Collection of Mr. and Mrs. Carl F. Kalnow
Collection of Robert Lyster
Manoogian Collection
Mr. and Mrs. David MacCallum
Munson Williams Proctor Arts Institute, Museum of Art
The New-York Historical Society
Peabody Essex Museum
Edwin and Sarah Pomphrey
Terra Foundation for the Arts
Vallejo Maritime Gallery
Erving and Joyce Wolf

Introduction: Silva Lined Clouds

John Wilmerding

THE SUBTLE, BEAUTIFUL ART of Francis A. Silva at last appears
to be receiving the full recognition and appreciation it deserves. A
generation ago, perhaps few more than a handful of curators, collectors,
and dealers knew his work, and then mainly the examples in museums,
such as Brooklyn, the Bostonian Society, and the New-York Historical
Society. Paintings elsewhere were seldom exhibited and rarely repro-
duced. While these are among his finest accomplishments, they seemed
at the time isolated and singular in the field, and neither the public
nor scholars had much of an idea of a larger and richer career.

In *A History of American Marine Painting*, the first survey of the
genre published in 1968, there is no mention of Silva (nor of William
Trost Richards, also highly valued today). That book largely concentrated on the early monographic research then underway on the major
figures of the later Hudson River School and luminism, such as Fitz
Hugh Lane, Martin Johnson Heade, and John F. Kensett. A few years
later the Whitney Museum's large survey exhibition in 1975, "Seascape
and the American Imagination," organized by Roger Stein, also neither
included nor mentioned Silva. In the accompanying book, Stein did
discuss and illustrate both the major figures of the period—Salmon,
Lane, Heade, Church, Kensett, Gifford—as well as many of the second-
level painters, like Aaron Draper Shattuck, John and James Hill,

[LEFT] *Boats at Anchor*, 1883 (detail)

William Bradford, James Suydam, William Stanley Haseltine, and A. T. Bricher, and even lesser names like Robert Swain Gifford and George Loring Brown.

Again linked with Bricher, Richards, and Haseltine, Silva did make an appearance in the large-scale exhibition, "American Light," at the National Gallery of Art in Washington, D.C. in 1980. Partly because of the ambitious scale, sweep, and quality of this monumental survey of American paintings of the mid-century period, these artists grouped under the rubric of luminism received new attention and interest. Silva now was better understood as both a second-generation and second-level luminist, one "occasionally capable of approaching the quality of the leading luminists." As the best examples of Lane, Heade, and others brought increasingly high prices on the market, and became steadily rarer to find, greater attention went to the works of Silva and his peers, and along with it an enhanced sophistication in discriminating his finest paintings from ordinary ones.

While we may yet not place Silva in the first tier of artists in market value or aesthetic accomplishment, he can certainly be viewed as one of the best of the larger group painting during the later portion of the century, more interesting and technically refined than either Shattuck or Bricher, and arguably on a par with W. T. Richards. By 1987 when *American Marine Painting* appeared in an expanded and revised edition,

both Richards and Silva were illustrated and discussed. In the meantime, John I. H. Baur, who is credited with first defining the term luminism in 1954, subsequently wrote a thorough article on Silva, describing him as "one of the most sensitive" artistic successors to Lane and Heade. And William Gerdts identified Silva as "an engaging painter [who] adopted luminist effects to good advantage." Contributing to this gradual process of reevaluation was the greater frequency of color reproductions of Silva's images appearing in books, catalogues, and articles. As works of comparable beauty to his view of *Schooner Passing Castle Island, Boston Harbor* (Fig. 10, Pl. 21) in the Bostonian Society became known, both critical and popular taste could appreciate the delicate nuances of his color gradations and the meticulous orchestration especially of his pinks, yellows, and lavenders for afternoon and evening scenes on the water.

Born in 1835, Silva went to school in New York, and enrolled in the Union army during the Civil War. Received knowledge has it that he was largely self-taught as an artist, though apparently he did have some early experience (as had Fitz Hugh Lane before him) as a sign painter. Quite possibly his earliest dated work is a watercolor of a coastal scene (Fig. 1, Pl. 1) painted in 1864. Like Lane's first efforts in printmaking and painting, it is tight and linear in rendering, in the conceptual tradition described by Barbara Novak. Yet for its modest size, the image has remarkable

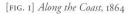

[FIG. 1] *Along the Coast*, 1864

strength, and unmistakably exhibits the personal character that would be refined in all of Silva's subsequent work. Together, the precise detailing, delicate coloring, and compositional clarity all belie the conventional notion of an untrained naïf, who abruptly started painting with this degree of confidence. Indeed, its closeness to the style of Lane and the earlier generation of luminists strongly suggests Silva had looked closely at those precedents. The New England setting of his work indicates Silva early and frequently visited the shorelines painted by Lane and others from the 1850s into the sixties and later. Moreover, Silva served in the same Union regiment as Sanford R. Gifford, himself painting light-filled landscapes and Civil War scenes at this time, and we have to wonder at the least if Silva did not benefit from some early instruction from this other luminist colleague.

What we do have now, thanks to the extensive research undertaken for this exhibition, is a much fuller picture of Silva's entire artistic life and enterprise: the amount and nature of his production, his extensive travels to paint up and down the Atlantic coast from the Chesapeake to Cape Ann, his submissions for exhibition at the National Academy of Design and especially his regular appearance at the American Watercolor Society throughout the 1870s and eighties, and some sense of his critical reception by patrons and the press. By the 1870s Silva was based in New York City, and in New Jersey by 1880. During the mid-eighties he was commuting back to New York, where he had a studio in the famed Tenth Street Studio Building, along with so many other significant American painters of his generation.

[FIG. 2] *Indian Rock, Narragansett Bay*, 1872

and uninspired repetitiveness. When the first-rate efforts are singled out, and our attention is concentrated on the exemplary pieces, as they are in this assemblage, we are in the presence of an artist capable of crisp design, telling details, and coloristic radiance.

Between his first dated work in 1864 and his death in 1886, current accounting records over one hundred and twenty-five dated oils and watercolors by Silva, and another five dozen undated pieces. The Peabody Essex Museum in Salem, Massachusetts, holds the largest collection of Silva items, consisting foremost of a typical finished oil painting and several dozen individual drawings, watercolors, and oil sketches. These latter include studies of water and waves, shorelines, and skylines, as well as several remarkable oil sketches of sunset clouds in the manner of Frederic Church's well known studies of twilight atmosphere executed throughout the 1850s. Another half dozen sketchbooks or clusters of studies give us rock drawings near Gloucester and, in a genre touch similar to Bricher, fashionably dressed women standing on ledges at the shore. One image specifically is identified as Salt Island, a favorite site also depicted by Fitz Hugh Lane in the late fifties and early sixties. Elsewhere we find harbor scenes and the island with Twin Lights, another Lane favorite.

One grouping of twenty marine sketches includes a watercolor of a beached shipwreck, which later led to a large

Not only his places of work but his subjects indicate that Silva had the frequent opportunity of looking at the work of both his older colleagues and contemporaries. For instance, Silva's painting of *Indian Rock, Narragansett Bay* of 1872 (Fig. 2, Pl. 13) is one of several made at that time: William Stanley Haseltine had made several drawings of the site around 1863, leading to a painting and a well-publicized engraving of the scene in *Picturesque America* in 1869. Two years later, Alfred Thompson Bricher painted one of his most beautiful large luminist canvases there. And of course, working in the area were others like James Suydam and Martin Johnson Heade. One of the stylistic idiosyncrasies that Silva shares with Heade was a predilection for numerous variations and repetitions of a particular view, sometimes refining his achievement in the process, and sometimes diminishing it through the dry

[FIG. 3] *Bass Rocks,* September 5, 1871

finished oil, beach scenes with boats nearby, a schooner in a harbor, and sailboats near shore, all subjects which would find their way into more complicated and ambitious canvases. One cluster of thirty-four drawings consists of various seascapes and one striking sheet depicting Sandy Hook, New Jersey, in five repeated strips of pencil sketches descending the page. There is a note with a scene of women at Bass Rocks, Cape Ann (Fig. 3, Pl. 50), and one of the beach near Point Judith, Rhode Island, familiar haunts respectively of Lane and Heade. Two final sketchbooks are devoted to the Rhode Island area and to the New Jersey shore, notably around Long Branch, this last with dates from the mid-1870s and 1880. Collectively, this rich material offers an intimate view of Silva's direct responses to nature and his working processes, over the several decades of his career and the many locations of his attention along the north and mid-Atlantic coastline.

Like most of his luminist and Hudson River School colleagues, Silva kept sketchbooks at hand, and drew regularly as he traveled, noting details of a view and possible compositional ideas. He frequently supplemented these with quick impressions in oil of light and atmospheric effects; in this regard he is closest to Richards and Church. But in particular, unlike Lane and Heade, who were primarily oil painters, Silva established himself along with Richards as equally accomplished in oil and watercolor. In both he favored the extended horizontal format, which he used for his beach views, often with sailboats off shore or a wrecked hull on the sand. Occasionally a standing figure or two looks to the distance; rowboats ride gently in the shallow water. At other moments boats of varied sizes idle in a cluster off a low point of land. Silva was different from Lane who virtually always kept to horizontal compositions; there are a small number of vertical format canvases, punctuated with the familiar sailboat set against a low horizon line. In keeping with a widespread practice of this generation of artists, Silva also periodically paired scenes of nature in sublime versus picturesque modes, with paintings of rough seas in contrast to those of becalmed waters and soft sunlit reflections. It is in this latter category that we tend to find his most memorable and evocative images.

Silva loved to paint sunrise and twilight, as well as the less frequent moonlight vista. He worked with rather gentle tonal effects across his open skies and the surfaces of a river or harbor, faceted by repeated ripples of reflected light. In a manner reminiscent of John F. Kensett's characteristic designs, Silva sometimes constructed strong asymmetrical balances of a vertical headland and a lateral expanse of water. At his most imaginative, he might play off a sweeping vista of a receding shoreline to one side with a concentrated massing of vessels with rising masts near the pilings of a dock on the other. In the juxtaposition of openness and density, lightness and dark, flatness and bulk, Silva could achieve a distilled sense of near abstract design and a compelling visual power.

[FIG. 4] *Off Newport, Rhode Island*, 1875

Appropriate for one who moved comfortably along the coast, whether ashore or on the water, Silva painted compositions of schooners at sea. But it is the more familiar human landscape of ordinary commerce, leisure, and coastwise travel he seemed to enjoy the most: the implications of an afternoon sail or an evening picnic, resting on the water when the wind has died down or the tide turned, the return to port and tying up at a wharf. At the same time, from his identifiable subjects and locations we can reconstruct a good deal of his career's itinerary. As Lane had before him, Silva painted a view of the America's Cup Race in 1875. Among the other sites he revisited and painted on several occasions were Boston and Gloucester harbors, Indian Rock and Narragansett Bay (Fig. 4), the Hudson River palisades and in particular Haverstraw and Tappan Zee, New York Harbor, and sections of the Long Island and New Jersey shores.

Remarkably, Silva's style and technique remained relatively consistent throughout his career. His works show a constancy of purpose and a confident hand in design and execution. At the same time, from the sixties to the eighties we can see how his career moves from its grounding in Ruskinian clarity of drawing to a later sensibility approaching the softer, more atmospheric touch of impressionism. His best mature paintings exude a mood and feeling of intimate tranquility. He rarely displayed the exuberant passions or intensity of color

pyrotechnics we see in Church during the 1860s. While Gifford may have been his first collegial precedent, Silva's place is perhaps best seen extending the stylistic legacy of Fitz Hugh Lane and John F. Kensett. This exhibition affords the satisfying and even unexpected pleasures of rediscovering and reevaluating a significant body of nineteenth-century American paintings. The accompanying research for this publication at last fills out the nature of Silva's life and art, while the cataloguing of his known works gives an indispensable reference framework for understanding the chronology of his career. Delivered from shadowy obscurity, Silva may now be seen in his own light.

Francis A. Silva (1835–1886), In His Own Light

Mark D. Mitchell

FRANCIS AUGUSTUS SILVA was a New Yorker. The son of an immigrant barber, he volunteered for military service even before the outbreak of the Civil War. Tough, opinionated, and resilient, the young captain emerged from that conflict to advance his nation's cause in art. From the very beginning of his artistic career, Silva turned to marine views for inspiration, and positioned his art firmly in the native aesthetic of American seascape now known as luminism. Over time, his interest in the classic forms of luminism ebbed, but his desire to advance American art endured. The young artist traveled along the east coast during the summer months, making preparatory studies for studio compositions that he completed in the winter. Silva's abbreviated career, curtailed by his death of pneumonia at age fifty-one, was marked by both his military service and his vantage on the American coast from New York. Despite his early demise, Silva contributed substantially to the iconography of the American seascape and to the rise of watercolor painting as a dedicated early member of the American Watercolor Society.

Silva's artistic range was broader than previous studies have suggested. With the advantage of a far larger record of the artist's work than has been available to date, we can see trends and themes emerge in high relief that had formerly been indiscernible. Two of the most

[FIG. 5] *Francis A. Silva,* April 1877, photograph, 4 x 3½ in., Private Collection

[LEFT] *Ten Pound Island, Gloucester,* 1871–72 (detail)

notable dynamics that appear are his evolving relationship to the Civil War's aftermath and his stylistic development over time from luminism toward a more dynamic realism. Several prevailing misconceptions about Silva's life and art will be confronted in order to grasp the nature of his artistic project more firmly. Admittedly, Silva's art is inconsistent in quality and negligible in terms of any direct influence on later artists. Nevertheless, his marginal status in the history of American art has hinged upon the misapprehension that Silva's work was consistently poor in quality. As the accompanying exhibition and color plates for this catalogue will demonstrate, no apologies are necessary. Silva's finest works stand on their own and demand greater recognition now that they have been identified. Redolent of the artist's and the nation's experience during the Civil War, Silva's art, perhaps more than that of any other contemporary painter, was imbued with his need to contend with recent history and then to move beyond it.

This essay is divided into three sections —biography, art, and reception—in order to give the reader a balanced perception of the artist, his development, and his work in context. That said, however, the majority of the text is dedicated to the study of Silva's paintings. The biographical discussion that begins the essay furnishes the reader with a sense of perspective on the artist's unusual military service and lifelong dedication

to country. The second portion of the text surveys Silva's *oeuvre* and is further parsed into three periods to reflect changes in his art over time. Although the discussion of Silva's painting commences with a definition of luminism derived from other artists, that description is intended only as a point of departure. Emphasis in the text is primarily placed upon Silva's paintings themselves, examining his work from the inside out rather than in relation to the work of other artists of the time. Finally, the essay will introduce the interrelated subjects of patronage and criticism of Silva's work during his lifetime. Despite his long-standing obscurity in the early twentieth century, a plight shared by many early American artists, Silva had reason to believe at several moments during his career that his artistic future was bright.

The contributions of this study to scholarship on Silva are several. The only substantial previous study of the artist was written over two decades ago with a relatively superficial understanding of his career. Not only does the accompanying catalogue increase the known record of Silva's work by an order of magnitude, but it also closes several gaps in our knowledge of his work. The most significant among these was filled by a major rediscovery in the collection of what is now the Peabody Essex Museum. Initially, Silva's preparatory works were divided by his daughter between what were then two institutions, the Peabody

Museum and Essex Institute. Although the Peabody collection was described in Marion Brewington's 1968 catalogue, the current study will be the first time that the wealth of the Essex collection has informed Silva scholarship. With the benefit of a computerized database of every work in the Peabody Essex collection, our grasp of Silva's career improves considerably. Beyond these new discoveries and the increased number of his final works that have been catalogued, the resulting analysis of Silva's work also differs from previous accounts. From the artist's concern with symbolic subject matter to his immense productivity in watercolor, the interpretation of Silva's work offered here will hopefully recast the discussion of his *oeuvre* and position in American art history.

Biography

Francis Silva inherited a legacy of art, war, and the sea that contributed significantly to the direction of his life. An 1867 record of the family's ancestry honors the artist's great grandfather, François Joseph de Lapierre, as a prominent leader and statesman of mid-eighteenth-century France. De Lapierre's son, François, was reportedly a childhood friend of Napoleon and later ascended to the rank of colonel in the French army. Recalled from a campaign in Italy by news of what would be his wife's fatal illness, Col. de Lapierre

was arrested by the revolutionary government for conspiracy, though he was never tried or charged. After four years in prison, de Lapierre was exiled to Lisbon where he disavowed his French citizenship and became an artist. He later remarried and moved to the Portuguese island of Madeira, off the coast of Africa. After de Lapierre's removal to Madeira, Napoleon purportedly offered to restore his rank and pay, but he refused. Soon thereafter he died in exile, never having restored his family's honor.

The colonel was survived by his wife and their two infant children. François Jean de Lapierre, the colonel's only son, entered the merchant marine at the age of fourteen, in spite of his mother's wishes to the contrary. She was painfully aware of the family's dishonor, and feared for his safety should he be recognized abroad. She told him the story of his father's exile, and instructed him to keep his history a secret and to change his name. François Jean apparently followed his mother's counsel and became Francis John Silva, adopting his aunt's surname. According to the 1867 text, written from Francis John's perspective, he "[k]ept the secret 37 years" after his departure from Madeira in June 1830.[1] Francis John became a barber in New York after his stint in the merchant marine and remained in the city for much of his life. The timing of Francis John's written narrative is itself remarkable, and points to the recuperation of the family's honor by the military service of his son, Francis Augustus, in the American Civil War. Whether or not the Silva family's sordid past was accurately remembered in 1867, that was how it was conveyed to young Francis Augustus, and it appears to have weighed heavily upon his later life.

Francis Augustus Silva was born on October 4, 1835 in New York, one of two children of Francis John's first marriage. Nothing is known of the artist's mother, except that she was born in New York City, according to the artist's death certificate. In addition to his one sibling, a brother, the artist later had two half-brothers and a half-sister from his father's subsequent remarriage. The origin of Francis Augustus' penchant for art may have lain in a youthful fascination with the mystery and intrigue surrounding the life of his paternal grandfather. Whatever its source, he manifested an early interest in the arts of design by showing at the American Institute's annual exhibitions for three consecutive years, beginning in 1848 at age ten. According to William DeCosta, one of Silva's informal biographers, the young artist showed "framed cards and pen drawings" and "earned amateur awards for this work."[2]

Although his parents apparently encouraged him in his precocious demonstrations of artistic talent, his father hoped to find a more practical trade for his oldest son. The boy was apprenticed to several trades before ending up with a sign painter. He worked in that trade until the outbreak of the Civil War in 1861, though accounts of his success in the profession vary. According to one obituary, Silva "painted signs so well, that he earned more wages than any other in the business, and after awhile bought out his time from his master and set up his studio and soon took a good rank among artists."[3] However apocryphal such a posthumous encomium may seem, Silva had established himself in business by early in 1859, when he appeared in the city directory for the first time at 619 Houston Street identified as a "painter."[4]

The commencement of Silva's artistic career, if only as a sign painter, coincided with his debut as a soldier in the mid-1850s. In April 1863, in the thick of the Civil War, Silva wrote to a Major General Hunter, probably David Hunter, in hopes of receiving a commission, and related the salient facts of his ill-fated military career to date.

> I served for some years as a private and a non-commissioned officer in the celebrated 7th Reg't. N.Y.S.M. [New York State Militia] (National Guard). At the outbreak of the present rebellion, I was commissioned First Lieutenant in the 9th N.Y. Vol. Infantry (Hawkins Zouaves) and commanded Company K of that Regiment from the day I was commissioned, until July

31st, 1861, when I was promoted to be Captain in the 1st N.Y. Vol. Infantry. I served until August 1862 when I was dismissed [*sic*] the service on account of a false muster against my name, made by my Colonel while I was sick in New York. I made application to the War Department to be restored. . . . The consequence was, I was restored to my command, "provided the vacancy was not filled." As my case had been delayed . . . the vacancy had been filled. Consequently, I was thrown out of a command.[5]

In May of 1862, during McClellan's famed Peninsula Campaign to seize the Confederate capital of Richmond, Silva fell ill with what John Dave, the regimental surgeon, diagnosed as "Miasmatic Disease," perhaps malaria. Silva was granted a leave of absence and apparently departed for New York. His superior officer, Colonel Dyckman, had Silva dishonorably discharged for desertion anyway, and the young artist-soldier spent the remainder of the war trying to regain a command after his successful reinstatement (and Dyckman's court-martial) in December 1862.[6]

A photograph of Silva in uniform (Fig. 6) was probably taken just after his commission as a captain in the First Infantry, New York, in July 1861. The photo portrays a proud young man at the height of his military career, and

[FIG. 6] *Captain Francis A. Silva, 1st Infantry, New York Volunteers*, c. 1861, photograph, 3½ x 2⅜ in., Private Collection

has fixed his image for art history to date. In many ways, that image of the artist as a young man is entirely appropriate. Baur described the "tinge of the military in Silva's character" that colored his personality throughout his life, but other, contemporary accounts privilege this

[FIG. 7] Winslow Homer (1836 – 1910) *The Briarwood Pipe*, 1864, oil on canvas, 42.8 x 37.5 cm., The Cleveland Museum of Art, 2002, Mr. and Mrs. William H. Marlatt Fund, 1944.524

aspect over any other, even at his death in 1886. Jervis McEntee recorded in his diary after attending the funeral that Silva was "dressed in his uniform and his hat and sword lay upon his coffin." McEntee further reminisced, "I always think of him as a soldier."[7] The effect of the Civil War upon Silva's development was signal. His early photograph offers insight both into the confidence of a twenty-five-year-old captain, and the lingering martial self-image that Silva preserved from that time until his death.

Some insight into Silva's military career and sense of duty may be gleaned from the regiments in which he served both before and during the war. His first regiment, the Seventh, founded in 1847, was also known as the "silk-stocking" regiment because its members bought their own uniforms and were notoriously self-conscious about such appurtenances.[8] His commission as a first lieutenant in Hawkins' Zouaves of the Seventh New York Volunteer Infantry, however, demonstrated that his commitment to service was more substantive than initial appearances suggest. These were the same flamboyant soldiers famously depicted by Winslow Homer in works such as *The Briarwood Pipe* (Fig. 7) of 1864. The American Zouaves sought to match their British counterparts of the Crimean War as examples of physical perfection, believing that their elaborate scarlet and blue costumes, based upon Arab dress, "signified toughness and physical courage."[9] This was the troop with which Silva associated himself at the onset of hostilities in 1861. He distinguished himself as one of their number, soon receiving his further promotion to captain, and remained in correspondence with his commanding officer long after the end of the war.[10]

Silva remained in New York City during his recuperation in 1862 and throughout the long wait for a military command thereafter. This period must have been difficult for the young soldier, who continued to work as an "ornamental painter" to earn his living. It was during this time, in 1864, that Silva painted his earliest dated work (Fig. 1, Pl. 1). The rediscovery of this luminous watercolor modifies our appreciation of the artist's early career substantially. Previous assessments relied upon New York directories and family tradition in placing the beginning of Silva's career as a fine artist in 1867 or 1868, respectively.[11] This work antedates that by at least three years, and documents his painterly maturation considerably before his appearance in New York directories as an artist in 1867.

The last year of Silva's military service, 1865, took him to Lynn, Massachusetts, where he was appointed army hospital steward.[12] Although only nominally military in nature, this new assignment restored him to active duty and resulted in an honorable discharge from service on November 16 of that same year. Silva's trip north was pivotal to his career as an artist, if not to his military promotion. His visit introduced him to the New England landscape—and seascape— for the first time, and probably inspired much of his later travel to the region as a practicing artist. Silva's military service also delimited his later geography. As an artist, he visited a host of scenic locations along the east coast, but rarely strayed far above Boston's North Shore or south of New Jersey.

After the conclusion of the war, Silva set up a studio in New York City in 1867, but traveled frequently. New York remained his professional center for the duration of his career, although he often chose to reside off Manhattan and commute to the city. Silva exhibited every year, virtually without exception, at the National Academy of Design, Brooklyn Art Association, and American Watercolor Society. Silva's participation in those organizations' exhibits and administration demonstrated his vested professional interest. He was elected to membership in the American Watercolor Society late in 1872 and likewise to the Artists' Fund Society in 1873. One of the greatest mysteries of Silva's life, however, remains his absence from the National Academy of Design's membership. Despite exhibiting at the Academy's annuals for nearly two decades, he was never made even an Associate Academician. Silva's aggressive criticism of the Academy late in his life may explain a certain coolness from the Academy, but does not explain why he was not admitted earlier in his career. In the absence of evidence, however, Silva's exclusion remains a matter of speculation.

Like many New York landscape painters, Silva traveled during the summers to accumulate source material for finished canvases that he completed after his return. A database of several hundred of the artist's sketches in the collection of the Peabody Essex Museum was created in the preparation of this exhibition and offers considerable detail about the artist's excursions. Although the Peabody

[FIG. 8] *Francis A. Silva*, n.d., photograph, 3½ x 2¼ in., Private Collection

Essex collection is doubtless only a partial record, it provides a far more comprehensive understanding of Silva's travels than had been available before. One issue that Silva's dated sketches do almost conclusively resolve is that the artist did not travel to Venice either in 1879 or 1883, if ever, as has been previously suggested.[13] On the contrary, as the artist advanced in his career, he appears to have stayed closer and closer to home. After his service in Lynn in 1865, the artist continued to visit Massachusetts and Rhode Island until 1873. During the mid-1870s, Silva remained mostly in the immediate vicinity of New York, spending time along the Hudson, on Long Island, in southern Connecticut, and in northern New Jersey. Finally, during the last portion of his career from the late 1870s onward, Silva almost exclusively explored the New Jersey coast from Hoboken to Atlantic City. Notably, these three phases in the artist's travel roughly paralleled the evolution of his painting style, as will be explored below.

Beginning in 1880, Silva moved his family to Long Branch, New Jersey, but continued to commute to New York until his death. The artist had married Margaret (Maggie) A. Watts in October 1868, and they had two children, Valentine and Marie Antoinette (Nettie). Very little is known about Maggie Watts, but their marriage in Keyport, New Jersey, suggests that the family's later move to nearby Long Branch may have been a return to her childhood home.[14]

Silva apparently recognized the economic advantages of working in Manhattan, however, and even rented a studio in the prestigious Tenth Street Studio Building from 1882 until his death in 1886.

Despite this apparently comfortable arrangement, Silva felt increasingly antagonized by the emergent artistic establishment of New York. During the 1880s, the city's prevailing aesthetic shifted definitively in favor of European Realism and Impressionism. Silva's resentment of the new bohemian class of modernists culminated in his vituperative 1884 article "American vs. Foreign-American Art," published in *The Art-Union*.[15] He condemned the returning students of European schools as "unpatriotic" and "narrow-minded." Not surprisingly, the former soldier grounded some of his criticism in the students' desire to avoid military service and their duty to country. Silva felt excluded from the fraternity of the American impressionists, and assailed their conservatism: "No one could paint, exhibit or earn a living if they [the impressionists] could prevent it, unless he conformed to their ideas of art."[16] Ironically, Silva's neighbor in the Tenth Street building was one of the greatest exemplars and proponents of this new school, William Merritt Chase.

Francis Silva died of double pneumonia at the home of a friend in New York on March 31, 1886 at age fifty-one, while still at the height of his artistic powers.[17] His passing was noted by the organizations of which he was a member, but failed to excite much interest in the artistic community in general. Two obituaries offer considerable insight into the abrasive public image that undoubtedly diminished his standing during a period in which personality was so important to artistic success.

He was a good man, full of fire, genial, determined, always trying to do right, truthful, honest, stubborn in his opinions, and in debate showed himself capable of maintaining his side of the argument with force, without any personal feeling; a good friend and a generous enemy, one who would tell you what he thought of you to your face, but never say a word about you behind your back to injure you in the eyes of another less generous than himself.[18]

A writer for the *New York Herald* was more circumspect, but the phrasing does not conceal a similar message: "He was a man of decided opinions, and at the meetings of the societies to which he belonged always expressed them in earnest and vigorous fashion."[19] Nevertheless, Jervis McEntee wrote of Silva's funeral, "I was pleased to see so many artists there [Thomas Waterman] Wood, [George Loring] Brown, [Thomas] Moran, [Arthur] Parton, [Lemuel] Wilmarth and others."[20] This group of artist acquaintances, if not friends,

furnishes significant information about Silva's artistic milieu and offers a point of departure for the examination of his *oeuvre*.

Art: Looking North, 1864 – 1874

The first decade of Silva's known artistic practice roughly coincided with the period of his greatest formal and thematic range. He experimented with a variety of forms, subjects, and media, seemingly questing for a personal solution to the received aesthetic mode of luminism and its implicit tenets. Several of his finest early works resonate with the classical mood of luminism, and this discussion will examine his response to that aesthetic as a foundation for his later departures. Concurrent with his more quintessentially luminist forays, Silva dabbled in different media and visual paradigms. He not only deployed more romantic (or "anti-classical," in Barbara Novak's parlance) formal tropes, including strong diagonals and unbalanced compositions, but also meaningfully expanded the range of themes that luminism conventionally embraced. Silva's simultaneous formal and thematic innovation recalibrated the luminist idiom to contend with the artist's (and the nation's) evolving concerns in the wake of war. Three themes emerge with particular frequency in his early production and merit direct scrutiny: rocky shorelines, lighthouses,

[FIG. 9] *Francis A. Silva*, n.d., photograph and ink, 6 x 4¼ in., Private Collection

[FIG. 10] *Schooner Passing Castle Island, Boston Harbor*, 1874

and the Hudson River. This characterization of Silva's work is necessarily reductive, but will be used to address several key preoccupations of his early career. Each of the three phases that roughly subdivide Silva's *oeuvre* has a characteristic subject or two that dominated his work. In this first period, the artist invoked time-honored themes, but imparted new, more poignant meaning to their iconographic elements within the context of the luminist idiom.

Silva's *Schooner Passing Castle Island, Boston Harbor* (1874, Fig. 10, Pl. 21) is undoubtedly the culminating example of his early work in the classic luminist style. Not only the style, but also the subject place this painting firmly in the tradition exemplified by the work of Gloucester native Fitz Hugh Lane (1804–1865). Silva's frequent travels to Cape Ann, Boston, and Narragansett

Bay during his first decade as an artist betray a strong northerly preference for the vistas and seascapes favored by Lane and other first-generation luminists. Lane's early death attracted considerable local attention, and his work was frequented exhibited in New England, particularly at the Boston Athenaeum, in the years around his death.[21] Silva probably saw Lane's work depicting the region and may even have met the artist himself while the younger man was still in service at the army hospital in Lynn, not far from Gloucester, in 1864. Lane's late work, such as his *Boston Harbor at Sunset* (late 1850s), incorporates a quality of suffused light similar to that in Silva's *Schooner Passing Castle Island*. Both paintings embody the full range of luminist principles exhaustively (if not exhaustingly) defined by Barbara Novak for the path-breaking 1980 exhibition entitled "American Light: The Luminist Movement, 1850–1875." That exhibition and its accompanying catalogue have framed subsequent discourse on the subject. Novak's contribution to the project was her essay "On Defining Luminism," in which she offered a methodical enumeration of the several "classical" aspects of luminist style.[22] Most of those qualities, from abstract geometry to the nature of the light, are exemplified by the major works of such canonical luminists as Lane and Martin Johnson Heade, but are equally employed in several of Silva's early compositions.

Foremost among the elements of luminism, so neatly outlined by Novak, is the one for which the aesthetic has received its latter-day rubric: light. Silva's treatment of light evolved considerably over the course of his career, but his early work is clearly indebted to the uncanny quality of light so characteristic of the works of first-generation luminists such as Lane and John Frederick Kensett. Among Kensett's famous "Last Summer's Work" before his death, he painted *Sunset on the Sea* (Fig. 11), a composition infused with a quality of light virtually identical to that which illuminated Silva's work of the same period. Likewise, the work of Silva's fellow veteran, Sanford R. Gifford, including the truly exceptional *Kauterskill Clove* (1862), furnishes a proximate source for Silva's treatment of light. Equally, the uncharacteristic upright orientation of Gifford's painting offers a suggestive precedent for Silva's later vertical compositions. Novak has described luminist light in appropriately abstract terms:

> Luminist light tends to be cool, not hot, hard not soft, palpable rather than fluid, planar rather than atmospherically diffuse. Luminist light radiates, gleams, and suffuses on a different frequency than atmospheric light. . . . Air cannot circulate between the particles of matter that comprise luminist light.[23]

The light in Silva's *Schooner Passing Castle Island* (Fig. 10, Pl. 21) embodies each of these qualities, and demonstrates his mastery of the classic luminist idiom. Silva's sun dissolves into a pool of rich purple, a color choice typical of his early work, but seemingly hyper-realistic. The effect approximates a haze across the sky, creating a uniformity of surface that flattens and evens the space above the horizon, and finally overwhelms the viewer with its sheer intensity. In many ways, the secondary properties that define the luminist mode flow naturally from this famed quality of light. Ultimately, however, light itself is the preoccupation of luminism, and Silva's canvas demonstrates his mastery of that elusive element.

[FIG. 11] John F. Kensett (1816 – 1872), *Sunset on the Sea*, 1874, oil on canvas, 28 x 41⅛ inches, Courtesy The Metropolitan Museum of Art, Gift of Thomas Kensett 74.3

Other characteristics of luminism that Novak isolates include emphases on abstract geometric forms and on the picture plane itself, imperceptible brushwork, quietude, and intimate size. Each luminist canvas, by Silva or any other artist, constitutes a unique balance among these several properties. With virtually mathematical precision, the separate elements in a particular painting add up to the art-historical abstraction called luminism. The wide range of works that are assembled under the aegis of luminism is at least somewhat explained by the varying balance of the parts, rather than an imprecise definition of the whole. Among Silva's early works, his *Off City Island, New York* (1870, Fig. 12, Pl. 2), *Evening in Gloucester Harbor* (1871, Pl. 6), *Sunrise, Boston Harbor* (1871, Pl. 10), *Boston Harbor* (1872), *Sunrise: Marine View* (c. 1873, Pl. 17), and *Sunrise at Barnegat Beach, New Jersey* (1875, Pl. 24) all fall

readily within the broad spectrum of "high style" luminism, to coin a term. While *Sunrise: Marine View* and *Evening in Gloucester Harbor* incorporate hot colors, they compensate with exaggerated emphasis on simplified abstract geometry and awareness of the picture plane. In *Evening in Gloucester Harbor*, Silva achieves those effects by strictly grouping the various schooners and pleasure boats along the horizon line. By disciplining his composition and simplifying its forms, the artist effectively orders the saturated, romantic chroma of the sunset and subjects it to the classicizing geometry characteristic of luminism.

Art historians generally acknowledge the 1870s as the decade of luminism's decline as a coherent aesthetic movement. Even during the later 1860s, however, Silva used repetition of particular iconographic elements to manipulate their significance and explore the boundaries of the classic

[FIG. 12] *Off City Island, New York*, 1870

luminist formula. In fact, Silva's primary themes often recurred throughout his career, but during certain periods he addressed one or more of those subjects more intensively and more frequently than the others. This discussion will employ those differing emphases as an interpretive device to suggest an evolution within Silva's art over time. In some cases, one theme takes up where another left off, as when the trope of a large rock on a shoreline was almost immediately supplanted by large shipwreck scenes in the mid-1870s. Both iconographic elements, the rock and the wreck, performed a similar task within the compositional structure, but the replacement of a large boulder with a shattered hull carries particular significance for an artist so profoundly affected by the Civil War. The patterns in Silva's treatments of different subject matter over time and the interactions between those subjects suggest that he was an independent spirit who worked methodically to advance the native school of art.

The first theme to appear regularly in Silva's *oeuvre* is the rocky coastline. This particular subject had a long history before he adopted it, but he brought a single-minded intensity to it that helped him to make the theme his own. Silva's fascination appears to have revolved around the interplay of the different conventional elements involved in the composition. Moving the ships closer to shore as in his *Coast of Maine* (1871), even if only through perspectival manipulation as in *Off the Gloucester Coast* (c. 1870), suggests danger, mortality, and vulnerability. Alternatively, removing the ships from a work like *Off Newport, Rhode Island* (1875, Fig. 4), leaves only the quiet, pre-Darwinian landscape of the ebb and flow of the tide and passing days. Silva's juggling of the differing elements within even the most conventional themes that he explored constitutes a kind of formal poetics. He used the elements of his compositions like phrases in a sentence, reordering them to achieve different meanings. This practice was inherent to much luminist art, and Silva carried on its use in a very literal form throughout his career. Even as the artist worked up a particular final composition, he often reorganized its major elements. His sketchbooks, in the collection of the Peabody Essex Museum, reinforce this interpretation of his practice. Although the seven books in the collection each contain a wide variety of subjects executed over a number of years and sketching trips, even a brief survey reveals that particular books were predominantly used for particular subjects. One book largely contains pencil sketches for the rocky shorelines, whereas another favors figure studies, and another includes most of his studies of buildings. To some degree, the artist appears to have separated out the individual aspects of his paintings and later reconstituted them into the final composition. Although seemingly naive and workmanlike, Silva's preparatory method was well suited to his poetic project.

[FIG. 13] *Calm Sunset*, 1873

[FIG. 14] *Moonrise*, n.d.

As Prof. Wilmerding points out in his introduction to this catalogue, Silva's early work exhibits a sharp linearity and specificity that is nearly Ruskinian. Despite such minute handling, found even in his earliest dated work *Along the Coast* (Fig. 1, Pl. 1), Silva never approached the topographical specificity of later Hudson River School painters such as David Johnson and Jervis McEntee. Although several of Silva's paintings depict specific locations, such as *Indian Rock, Narragansett Bay* (1872, Fig. 2, Pl. 13), they nevertheless treat the subjects more broadly than most other artists of the period, and they consequently privilege the symbolic over the specific. Over time, the symbolic appears to have

[FIG. 15] *Women Walking along the Shore*, n.d.

become only more important to Silva's art. Within the context of the rocky coastline theme, that evolution manifested itself in the move toward an ever-larger single rock, in lieu of a full coastline fraught with continuous peril. The large boulder adopted iconographic significance apart from the coast, and even became the primary subject of several compositions such as *The New England Coast* (c. 1870), *Calm Sunset* (1873, Fig. 13), *Moonrise* (n.d., Fig. 14), and *Women Walking along the Shore* (n.d., Fig. 15). The single rock does not threaten, but simply endures. The stone defies waves and weather to move it or wear it down. Often situated on a beach or protruding from the waves, the symbolic stone embodies longevity. In a nation with few anchors after the war, Silva's massive and distinctive boulders offer the qualities of stability and steadfastness that the artist sought for his nation and for himself. Although these were by no means Silva's finest canvases from his early

period, this kind of experimentation led to greater successes in later years.

The second of Silva's early themes was also redolent of war's aftermath: the coastal lighthouse. These defensive, protective beacons guarded against the dangers of the shoreline's rocks and shoals. Several of Silva's paintings of lighthouses draw a direct parallel between these man-made beacons and their natural equivalents, the sun and moon. *Sunrise: Marine View* (c. 1873, Pl. 17) is an outstanding example. The shaft of sunlight reflected off the water is so intense as to defy credulity, echoing the vertical shaft of its reflection upon the lighthouse's tower. In their geometric simplicity, both pillars of light support their respective beacons. *Ten Pound Island, Gloucester* (1871–72, Pl. 12) is an equally clear expression of Silva's visual metaphor, while *Moonrise* (1872) and *Calm Sunset* (1873, Fig. 13) operate similarly. Wayne Craven has written of *Sunrise: Marine View* that it is "painted in such a way as to suggest a hushed, unhurried world, which served as an antidote to the super-energized, dynamic, industrialized place America had become. . . ." [24] While Craven's assessment is accurate in the sense that Silva focused more often upon sail than steam, the artist was not shy about depicting steamboats (witness his *Ferryboats near the Battery* (Fig. 16) featuring two steamboats as the central subjects) and the lighthouses that he painted were new fixtures that depended upon new lens and lamp technologies to improve their performance. These were not old-world outposts, but ultra-modern technological achievements standing in the face of the elements to guard American commerce from the hazards of travel at night and in inclement weather. In a sense, the lighthouses also shared the mute heroism of Silva's large boulders, as both endured the ravages of nature impassively.

Silva's paintings are not anti-modern simply because he embraced the native luminist aesthetic rather than a more cosmopolitan European mode. An artist as intrigued by light as Silva would naturally have been attracted by the technical achievements of American lighthouses, as this series of works attests. The compositional arrangement of his 1869 *An August Morning at Cohasset, Massachusetts* also strongly indicates an interest in photography, particularly stereoscopy. (The stereoscope was the nineteenth-century precursor to 3-D glasses; the viewer looks through a pair of lenses that superimpose two similar images of the same

[FIG. 16] *Ferryboats near the Battery*, 1874

[FIG. 17] *The Husdon River Looking toward the Catskills,* 1871

scene to create the impression of three-dimensionality.) The strong foreground, regular spatial recession of the three peninsulas projecting from the left edge, and the broad swaths of seemingly unde-marcated water activated only by a small rowboat that appears to hover in space collaborate to invest the painting with a three-dimensional quality very close to stereo photography when viewed from several yards away. Stereoscopy was in its heyday around 1870. The medium was so pervasive, in fact, that it would have been truly extraordinary were Silva unaware of it. His decision to invoke stereo aesthetics was consistent with the interests of both luminist painters and photographers of the period. Weston Naef has probed the relationship between luminism and photography in his essay for the "American Light" exhibition entitled, "'New Eyes'—Luminism and Photography."[25] Several samples of landscape stereographs similar to Silva's *An August Morning* illustrate Naef's

essay, including Seneca Ray Stoddard's *Moonlight on Lake George* (c. 1875–80). Silva's interest in the modern innovations of lighthouses and photo aesthetics participate in the artist's larger concern with light and the nature of vision. Far from being intentionally nostalgic, Silva's aesthetic inquiries and subject matter point to a highly modern sensibility and fascination with new technology, particularly that which related to light.

By far the most famous of Silva's themes from this early period was not formal, but geographic: the Hudson River. There are a number of genuinely exquisite examples in this series, several of which are included in this exhibition. *The Hudson River Looking toward the Catskills* (1871, Fig. 17), *On the Hudson, Nyack* (1871, Pl. 9), *Kingston Point, Hudson River* (c. 1873), *Sunrise at Tappan Zee* (1874, Pl. 22), *The Hudson at Tappan Zee* (1876, Pl. 26), and *On the Hudson River, Nyack* (n.d., Pl. 43) share a number of the distinctive properties of Silva's work in the early 1870s. The series also contains several of Silva's earliest efforts in vertical format, including *View on the Hudson River* (1876, Pl. 27) and *Schooner on a River* (n.d., Pl. 46). In recent years, the Hudson River group has grown to be synonymous with the name Francis Silva, despite its relative brevity and transitional nature within his *oeuvre*. Works such as *On the Hudson River, Nyack* incorporate both the diffuse light and palette range (though more muted) of his earlier compositions, but applied to the quintessential nineteenth-century landscape subject. Increasingly, however, as in the Brooklyn Museum's 1876 *The Hudson at Tappan Zee* (Pl. 26), both the light and palette are transformed, creating the brilliant clarity and less saturated colors that typified the artist's second phase. Perhaps because of the transitional nature of this moment in Silva's career, his Hudson River scenes are among his most charming and effective early works. Instead of over-reaching his limits, the artist incorporated the most nuanced elements of his early work (even an occasional lighthouse and boulder), but had not yet embraced the colder, less forgiving light of the later 1870s. The correspondence between the Hudson River and the quality of these paintings is virtually inexplicable, as they stand apart aesthetically from his other work of the early 1870s. Perhaps the phenomenon is best explained simply as a serendipitous consequence of time and geography, of Silva's concurrent artistic maturation

and awareness of his Hudson River School predecessors on their turf. Just as the Boston and Cape Ann landscape evoked an appreciation of Lane's luminism, perhaps the Hudson itself inspired Silva's next evolution.

The work that Silva produced during his first period readily falls within the parameters of luminism. Perhaps susceptible to Lane's influence because of an early exposure to the older artist's work, the young veteran frequently returned to the Boston area to accumulate source material for his compositions. Luminism was a balancing act for all of its practitioners, but Silva apparently interpreted the luminist equation more literally than most. Frequently reworking similar compositions on identical themes to alter or refine their meaning, Silva began to address a particularly favored subject virtually to the exclusion of others. Although his intense examination of a single theme rarely endured more than five years, his early production suggests a broad range of interests that was gradually eclipsed by his successive preoccupations. Silva's early concentration on the tropes of rocky coasts and lighthouses further suggests a symbolic, almost biographical dimension to his practice of art. As he strove to establish a distinctly personal luminist vernacular, he wrestled with war's influence on himself and the nation at large. Those concerns would come ever more explicitly to the fore during the second period of Silva's career, the later 1870s.

Art: Icons of Loss, 1874 – 1880

The wreck of the schooner *Progress* on July 4, 1874 inspired Silva as nothing before. The double symbolism of the vessel's name and the date of its demise exerted a magnetic attraction upon the artist. He returned to the wreckage several times for well over a month, depicting it from sundry angles and under varying weather conditions. Even the Peabody Essex Museum's irregular survey of the artist's preparatory sketches contains at least four substantial watercolor studies of the schooner's remains (Figs. 19 and 20). Those four are known because they are

specifically titled by the artist, but any number of other studies from this unusually well-documented period may depict this scene. Silva's nearly obsessive examination suggests an ardent desire to mine the uncanny symbolism of the wreck. He painted at least two exhibition-scale compositions of the scene in the following year, of which *The Schooner "Progress" Wrecked at Coney Island, July 4th, 1874* (1875, Fig. 18, Pl. 23) represents one of the artist's greatest aesthetic and symbolic achievements.

The shipwreck motif in American art of the mid-nineteenth century was

[FIG. 18] *The Schooner "Progress" Wrecked at Coney Island, July 4th, 1874*, 1875 well established by the time Silva painted his *Schooner "Progress."* The ancestry of the ship of state metaphor is even more ancient, dating as far back as the writings of Sophocles. Silva himself had already painted several shipwreck scenes before arriving on the beach at Coney Island. With his final composition, however, Silva encapsulated his own ambivalence toward his nation in the midst of its painful Reconstruction. Progress had been a defining staple of American pride since the founding. Asher B. Durand's large 1853 paean to the national spirit was even titled *Progress* and showed the gradual, inexorable expansion of the American people westward.

In contrast, Silva's *Progress* has slammed headlong into the beach, its skeletal remains reaching upward toward the incongruously peaceful sky. Silva takes a low vantage point, causing the timbers of the ruined hull to penetrate the sky. The compositional arrangement and recognizable prow of the schooner's hull driven into the ground are strikingly anthropomorphic and invoke the shocking photographic portrayals of corpse-strewn Civil War battlefields produced by Mathew Brady's studio. That allusion would become even more overt in later compositions such as *A Summer Day on the Coast* (1882, Pl. 35). Implicit in the array of ships at the horizon in Silva's *Schooner "Progress"* is a nostalgic sense of a bygone era, like that described by Craven in relation to the artist's earlier

work. Here, however, Silva has discernibly altered the character of light and color in his composition, maneuvering toward a clarity and brilliance previously unknown in his work. Although he did not actively pursue the shipwreck theme for another five years, Silva's artistic response to the wreck of the *Progress* inaugurated a new phase in his aesthetic development.

As mentioned earlier, the shipwreck motif in Silva's work, particularly the *Progress*, served the same compositional function as the large boulders of his earlier seascapes. In none of Silva's later shipwrecks do we find a rocky coastline upon which the ship was destroyed. Instead, we customarily find a sandy beach, with a wreck's decaying form as the only sign of a narrative. Despite their compositional similarity, however, the shift from geological to human events suggests a profound change in the symbolic function of the looming form. In lieu of a vast boulder able to defy the elements, Silva places the broken, though recognizable pieces of a man-made ship—not only a ship, but in the case of the *Progress* a schooner, symbolic of the age before steam. Unlike the vast rocks of *The New England Coast* or *Calm Sunset* (Fig. 13), the shipwrecks generally suggest deterioration. Both *Coastal Sunset* (1874, Pl. 20) and the *Schooner "Progress"* show signs of such decay as waves disperse the shattered timbers in the former, and lichen and water visibly penetrate the latter.

Only a spot of bright, white paint remains on the surface of the *Progress*, suggesting its former glory.

There is a sharp difference in emphasis between the final version actually entitled *The Schooner "Progress"* and another permutation of the theme that is simply titled *Approaching Storm* (c. 1875).[26] In the latter variant, the schooner's wreckage has sunk considerably lower into the sand, more akin to the effect of Silva's July 28, 1874 study (Fig. 19, Peabody Essex Museum, Acc. No. M8871-B3.31) than that of August 15 (Fig. 20, Peabody Essex Museum, Acc. No. M8871-B3.18), upon which he based the *Schooner "Progress."* Both final compositions are the same size, but Silva seems to have appreciated the greater symbolic value of the *Schooner "Progress,"* and titled the works accordingly. Not only does the hull rise higher out of the sand by virtue of the artist's vantage point in the *Schooner "Progress,"* but he has also cleaned up the rest of the wreckage on the beach, endowing the intact prow with even greater visual emphasis. Silva's continual adjustment of his compositions even in their final versions demonstrates his desire to refine continually and improve each work. The intensity with which he studied the *Progress* and worked up his final composition offers a microcosmic sampling of his work on the different themes that comprise his *oeuvre*.

[FIG. 19] *Coney Island, July 28, 1874*

[FIG. 20] *Coney Island, August 15, 1874*

David Miller has offered the only critical study of Silva's place in American art history to date, and his argument revolves around the shipwreck theme as depicted in various works including Silva's *Coastal Sunset* (1874, Pl. 20) and *Schooner "Progress."* [27] Unfortunately, Miller's essay suffers from underanalysis of specific works and falls frequently into misguided generalization. He argues, for example, that the archetypal "futurity" of the American landscape "dissolves" in these shipwreck scenes, despite the ships sailing prominently under clement skies in the backgrounds of both of Silva's works. [28] The contribution of Miller's essay to the study of Silva's career, and specifically the *Schooner "Progress,"* is his analysis of the several tensions at play, most notably that between religious and secular spheres in the later nineteenth century. During the Civil War, "Northern clergymen spurred aggression toward the South by casting the war as a crisis, an Armageddon, in America's mission to redeem the world for Christ." [29] The nineteenth-century notion of progress that Silva's ante-bellum schooner symbolizes was the hallmark of that redemptive mission.

According to Miller, the change underway in luminist painting was from its roots in a highly religious, cyclical vision of landscape and history into a post-Darwinian, linear mode based in natural history. Miller's argument unravels in its details, but successfully explicates,

though not directly, the interactions between Silva's boulders and his shipwrecks. Their massive forms serve similar compositional functions as they are often close in general outline, but their iconography is difficult to reconcile without an appreciation of the post-war schism between religious and secular views of human history. Although Silva's religious disposition is not known, the iconographic elision of sacred and secular in his paintings at this watershed in his artistic career suggests some degree of awareness of the terms of the contemporary debate. Thus, while Miller's essay misfires in the specifics, he nevertheless offers an important interpretive tool for the study of Silva's iconography.

The year 1875 also witnessed the ascendancy of Silva's practice of watercolor. Even though his first dated work was a watercolor, and he was eulogized in the *Magazine of Art* exclusively as a watercolorist, Silva's watercolors are today the least known of his works. John Baur made virtually no mention of Silva's work in the medium, and most subsequent scholarship has continued to ignore their significance. By the 1880s, Silva was only exhibiting watercolors at the Brooklyn Art Association annuals. Once again, however, without a broad survey of Silva's production, there would be no way to assess objectively the artist's turn to watercolor in the mid-1870s—except one. The exhibition catalogues of the American Watercolor Society offer both numeric evidence for Silva's increasing interest and also illustrate several of his works that are now unlocated.

Like Silva's works in the medium, however, the history of the Society has attracted only minimal art-historical attention to date.[30] The Society was founded in 1866 and collaborated with the National Academy of Design in its winter exhibitions. By 1873, when Silva was elected to membership, the Society had already established a moderate reputation, and commanded a fair amount of consideration among critics and patrons. Nevertheless, Silva's use of the medium remained primarily preparatory for his oils. He only exhibited a few works each year for the first three years of his membership in the Society. In 1876 alone, however, Silva exhibited a total of twelve finished watercolors, double the number that he had exhibited to that point combined, ushering in the new era of his artistic practice. The medium's properties were tailored to his aesthetic of the later 1870s, and his oils from the period often look more like watercolors than vice versa.

The *Schooner "Progress"* shares several of the distinctive stylistic properties of Silva's watercolors of the late 1870s, despite their differences in subject matter, and suggests the *Progress* catalyzed his stylistic evolution. No simple explanation presents itself for the lighter, brighter mood of Silva's paintings after 1874. Instead of the diffuse, colored light that epitomized his early work, Silva's depictions of beaches and ports during this period are distinctive for their crystalline clarity. Although the *Schooner "Progress"* is the most exemplary representation of this new aesthetic mode, numerous other known works from the period, in both oil and watercolor, incorporate its sharp, limpid light.

The ramifications for the overall effect of Silva's canvases were remarkable as well. As described initially, many of Silva's atmospheric and colorist effects derived from the quality of light that he depicted. *Dunes* (1875, Fig. 22), *View on the Hudson River* (1876, Pl. 27), *View near New London, Connecticut* (1877, Pl. 29), *Barnegat Bay, New Jersey* (c. 1877, Fig. 27), *Fishing Boats on Jamaica Bay* (1878, Fig. 21) *Great South Bay off Fire Island* (1879, Fig. 23), *On the New Jersey Coast* (1879, Fig. 48), and *An Old New*

[FIG. 21] *Fishing Boats on Jamaica Bay*, 1878

39

[FIG. 22] *Dunes*, 1875

England Seaport (1880) all share this new quality of light. Silva did continue to paint compositions in his more traditional, light-suffused aesthetic on occasion, but this new development brought with it certain advantages. In particular, it permitted Silva to explore a fuller range of his palette. Even in the simplified, nearly abstract *Dunes*, he experimented with a more nuanced range of local color. The resulting sense of detail and specificity brought Silva closer to Ruskinian aesthetics than he had ever been before, or ever would be again. This more complex color aesthetic, not dominated by any single color like the purple that appeared so frequently in his earlier work, demonstrated Silva's increasing mastery over his palette and his desire to put that mastery to use. *The Schooner "Progress"* paved the way for this limpid aesthetic to dominate the artist's *oeuvre* for the latter portion of the decade.

Depicting the beaches and placid harbors of the area around New York, Silva's work of the late 1870s changes remarkably in tone as well as style. Divested of the cumbersome cadmiums and hulking forms of large boulders in the shoreline, his compositions temporarily vacillated between being divine elegies and domestic, humanized representations of the landscape, and favored the latter. Man has little to fear from weather or other natural threats in these works, and they rarely contain any overt reference to danger, such as a storm or wreck. When a ship's remains are shown, they have been dismantled not by nature, but by men. Silva's *View near New London, Connecticut* (1877, Pl. 29) depicts a wrecker's dock and adjacent beach strewn with the vestiges of a decommissioned ship. This beguiling scene balances the elements of organized destruction with a man fishing, a nearby home, and the city of New London visible across the inlet. Here the ruins suggest a controlled passage of time, organized by the rational will of man instead of the arbitrary wrath of god. Silva's message in this work is exceptionally clear, and contrasts sharply with many works created both before and after this phase in his career. These were the halcyon days.

These idylls benefit remarkably in clarity, depth, and brilliance from the artist's increased use of watercolor. Silva's appreciation of the properties of the medium enabled him to explore the use of space more actively in his work and to create more dynamic arrangements. The distinctive portrayal of air and wind is one of the most notable attributes of Silva's painting of the period. Although he literally colored the light and made it visible in his earlier, light-filled compositions, his work in the late 1870s shows the presence of air less directly, by representing its effects. Focus shifts in works such as *America's Cup Race* (1875–76), *The Hudson at Tappan Zee* (1876, Pl. 26), *Sunset at Cape Ann* (1876), *After the Equinoctial, off Sandy Hook* (1879), and *Great South Bay off Fire Island* (1879, Fig. 23) to the tension in the ships' rigging that the wind produces. *Coastal Schooners–Moonrise* (1874, Pl. 19) is a particularly strong example, because the ship travels laterally across the composition, and its sails are thereby rendered almost invisible to the viewer as they strain to tow the schooner along. With only the ropes, masts, and contours of the sails discernible, the resulting crisp,

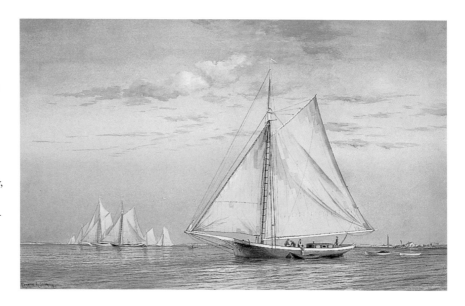

[FIG. 23] *Great South Bay off Fire Island*, 1879

linear geometry is strongly reminiscent of Silva's first dated work, *Along the Coast* (1864, Fig. 1, Pl. 1). The contrast in proficiency between the two paintings is considerable. Nevertheless, the works share an emphasis upon geometry that firmly establishes it as one of the artist's enduring shibboleths.

In 1879, Silva drew and painted several works that depict Venice. The arrival of this seemingly anomalous subject in Silva's art toward the end of the second phase of his career more likely signaled a desire to experiment with something new, rather than an urgent desire to travel abroad. In 1884, he publicly lambasted American artists who traveled abroad in search of training and inspiration. In an article entitled "American vs. Foreign-American Art," Silva scoffed:

[FIG. 24] Sanford R. Gifford (1823 – 1880) *Venetian Sails: A Study*, 1873, Oil on canvas on masonite, 13 3/8 x 24 inches, Courtesy Washington University Gallery of Art, St. Louis, Bequest of Charles Parsons, 1905

[FIG. 25] *Venetian Scene*, c. 1879

Young men who might make good merchants or tradesmen are sent to Paris by mistaken friends; they learn the mechanical part of art, and wonder when they return, at the success of some painter who has not had the benefit of instruction in a good school, but whose pictures are full of an art feeling which they not only do not possess, but have no conception of. [31]

His aggressive stance toward foreign influence suggests that even his few Venetian scenes might border upon the hypocritical, but his essay is perhaps better seen as an artist's bridling at the contemporary fashion for foreign aesthetics than a blanket condemnation of all things European. Over time, his nativist opinions appear to have hardened, and doubtless won him few friends. Venice was, however, an enormously popular destination for American artists, particularly those interested in the study of light. At least two of Silva's friends went to Venice in the 1870s and 1880s, George Loring Brown and Thomas Moran. Gifford also traveled there, and his *Venetian Sails: A Study* (1873, Fig. 24) is remarkably similar in palette and composition (even if it is horizontal) to Silva's two known finished canvases, both entitled *Venetian Scene* (1879 and c. 1879, Fig. 25).

Silva's desire to emulate the canvases of his peers suggests a desire to explore and internalize the aesthetic mode then prevalent among Americans in Venice, such as Gifford. Margaretta Lovell has characterized this mode, in terminology that she borrowed from literary critic Northrop Frye, as "low mimetic."[32] In this idiom, the artist (or author) creates a visual narrative that is specifically "nonheroic." That is to say, citing Frye, "the protagonist in this mode is 'superior neither to other men nor to his environment, the hero is one of us: we respond to a sense of his common humanity, and demand from the poet the same canons of probability that we find in our own experience.'"[33] It was entirely appropriate, then, that Silva adopted a Venetian aesthetic common among American practitioners of the time that was also compatible with his second period style and iconography. After the *Progress*, there are no more (known) subjects of such historic and symbolic magnitude.

By choosing Venice, in particular, as his subject, Silva embraced idiomatic and mnemonic complexity in line with the *Schooner "Progress,"* despite the absence of such a central symbolic element in his subsequent seaside works of the period. The artist confronted what Lovell has characterized as the "Ozymandiazs Problem," after Percy Shelley's famous poem. The artist and viewer encounter in the work, like Shelley's traveler, the remains of a past civilization, seeing only the proud inscription upon a monument's pedestal long after the monument itself has turned to dust.

> "My name is Ozymandias, king of kings; / Look on my works, ye Mighty, and despair!" / Nothing beside remains. Round the decay / Of that colossal wreck, boundless and bare / The lone and level sands stretch far away.[34]

The analogy to Silva's wrecked *Progress* is clear, as the ship itself was an homage to that national "king of kings."[35] All that remains of the once proud ideal, however, is a name and a few crumbling fragments. If we follow Lovell's argument about works depicting Venice— and, by extension, Silva's *Schooner "Progress"*—to its conclusion, the representations of Venice by American artists wrestled with the painful memory of their own nation's recent tumult by displacement. In the afterglow of the recent Civil War, American artists felt a profound attraction to Venice as a place of both memory and historical amnesia. In their works, artists such as Silva contended with the processes of national memory and with the futility of erecting monuments to the past.[36]

At the end of Silva's second period, we find a key to interpreting his work throughout the second period and beyond. Beginning with a perceptible withdrawal from the transcendental quality of luminism he had previously practiced, Silva's contention with the significance of the schooner *Progress* precipitated the change in his artistic mode away from contemplation of the divine and toward human events. The last three lines of Shelley's poem cited above could very easily be a description of the beach scenes that Silva painted during the late 1870s. The pedestal of Ozymandias, of course, finds its own equivalent in the ruined mass of the *Progress*. Silva's tentative and short-lived experimentation with Venetian subjects provides useful interpretive insight into his second period, but also furnishes a sense of continuity as the artist vigorously pursued the disparate subjects of shipwrecks and domestic scenes in the final period of his career.

Art: Conflict in the 1880s

In 1880, Silva moved his family to Long Branch, New Jersey. For the remainder of his career, he would focus his attention on the New Jersey shore. Although he continued to travel to nearby cities in search of subjects, he remained much closer to home than he had in earlier years. Over time, his geographic focus had crept steadily southward. Beginning in Cape Ann, Boston, and Narragansett during the 1860s, he soon shifted his attention to the Hudson River, Connecticut shore, and Long Island for most of the 1870s. Finally, his peregrinations led him to northern New Jersey where he settled, a move that accompanied a noticeable change in his art once again. Most immediately, the ascendancy of two familiar themes from his earlier career epitomized his final years: sunsets and shipwrecks. Silva had never completely ceased to depict either theme, but they constituted a minority of his production during the interim. Between these two themes, however, lay a considerable intellectual space, and the artist appears to have been of two minds about what direction to pursue. Either because he felt that they were better compositions or simply because they sold better, the shipwrecks dominated his exhibition entries, and were consistently his choice from among his own works to reproduce in catalogues and magazines. This discussion will chart the evolution of each of these themes in Silva's work of the 1880s, and consider their ambivalent interactions in light of the artist's increasing hostility toward the impressionists who dominated the New York art world at the time.

Silva's resentment of the "conservative" impressionists can be documented throughout this period in his career. His disaffection initially appeared in 1880, when he copied an article on "Dandyism" into his sketchbook from the pages of *Scribner's Monthly*.[37] The article begins with Thomas Carlyle's definition of a dandy as "a clothes-wearing man—a man whose trade, office and existence consists in the wearing of clothes." In the passage that Silva transcribed, the article's author wrote extensively on dandyism in art. Of course, beginning in 1882, one of Silva's neighbors in the Tenth Street Building was arguably the single most famous American dandy of the period (after Whistler), William Merritt Chase. Small wonder that Silva's attacks became increasingly venomous, culminating in his 1884 article "American vs. Foreign-American Art." That 1884 essay was Silva's first tentative step into the public sphere, and the tone of his writing suggests that he had nursed his resentment for several years before he expressed it in print. Silva was well known for his prickly attitude at meetings of the societies of which he was a member, but to publish an attack suggests progressive disenfranchisement from those institutions where he had previously held sway. When Silva then published the first

history of the American Watercolor Society in 1885, he framed its founding and evolution as a bastion of aesthetic liberalism, implicitly opposed to other institutions that were certainly not to remain nameless, such as the National Academy of Design. As the 1880s progressed, Silva's own art reflected his profound ambivalence toward the ascendant oligarchy of the impressionists, and the thematic schism in his art of the period roughly correlates to his reluctant modernism.

The resurgence of sunsets in Silva's art should not be interpreted merely as a regression. Firstly, his sunsets of this period, most of which date roughly from 1879 to 1883, differ substantively from the earlier, luminist works like *Evening in Gloucester Harbor* (1871, Pl. 6) or *Sunrise: Marine View* (c. 1873,

[FIG. 26] *Evening*, 1881

Pl. 17) in the quality of their light. No longer does the diffuse light pervade the landscape. Instead, in sunsets like *Twilight along the River* (1879, Fig. 49), *Low Tide* (1880, Pl. 33), *Evening* (1881, Fig. 26), and *By the Seaside, New Jersey Shore* (1883), Silva employed a broader range of color locally in the sky and more actively emphasized silhouettes to create a sharp contrast between the tranquillity of the foreground and the drama of the sky. Contrast now plays a far greater role in the sunset than compositional unity or light. As has been discussed in relation to Silva's works of the later 1870s, changing attitudes toward divine omnipotence in the wake of the Civil War offer a likely explanation for the artist's withdrawal from the highest pitch of transcendentalism within the luminist aesthetic. In making this change, Silva positioned his works within a much larger movement in art and society taking place toward the close of the century.

More noticeable perhaps than the change in quality of light is the difference in subject matter portrayed in these later sunsets. Replacing the lighthouse iconography are domestic scenes of houses along the shore, usually with small piers or beaches where boats are tied up or moored. Although lighthouses imply the protective embrace of home and safety, they also suggest warning and danger. Substituting hearth and home for the lighthouse echoes changes in Silva's life as well. With a wife and two young children to support, Silva was apparently much affected by home life. His sketchbooks from the period show a notable increase in the presence of figures. His daughter, Marie Antoinette, was a particularly favored sitter as she often appears in Silva's sketchbooks at the Peabody Essex. She apparently accompanied him on his sketching trips on occasion and was a willing subject for his art. Silva's youthful wanderlust appears to have largely abated by the 1880s, and his family and home inspired him with greater frequency.

Domestic life may also have appealed to Silva's nativism. Despite naming his daughter Marie Antoinette, a rather remarkable nod to the French *ancien régime*, Silva remained profoundly patriotic, and increasingly proletarian. Throughout his vitriol of the mid-1880s ran the refrain of nativism and borderline xenophobia. The hearth had long been equated with Americanism in popular visual culture. In *Seabright from Galilee* (1880), Silva even includes a small child playing along the shore, but this toddler by no means represents the same socio-economic class as the figures in his earlier beach scenes, such as *A Summer Promenade along the Beach at Coney Island* (1870, Pl. 3) and *The Beach at Long Branch, New Jersey* (c. 1869, Fig. 31). During his later years, Silva dramatically shifted his subjects toward an idealized vision of the working class, especially fishermen. *Barnegat Bay, New Jersey* (c. 1877, Fig.

[FIG. 27] *Barnegat Bay, New Jersey*, c. 1877

27), *The Fisherman's Home* (1879), and *Evening* (1881, Fig. 26) apparently depict the homes of fishermen by juxtaposing ship and house. The quietude of *Evening* and *Low Tide* (Pl. 33), among others, immediately evokes a sense of rest after a day of work. Labor, too, would become a central refrain for Silva in his writings, as he cited honest hard work as the solution to dandyish bohemianism.

If labor was the cure, then dandyism was the disease. To Silva, impressionism was artistic dandyism, but even he was not fully immunized. During the 1880s, he returned not only to the sunset theme, but also to the wreck and its companion, the storm. These themes, domestic sunsets and romantic wrecks may appear initially to be irreconcilable, but they most likely simply represent opposing sides of the same coin. In both subjects,

the artist was responding to the threat posed by impressionism. In the first, Silva returned to the classically American idiom of luminism further sanctified by elements of family and labor. In the second, he struggled to come to grips with newer stylistic developments on his own terms. Baur has celebrated *A Summer Afternoon at Long Branch* (1885, Fig. 57) as "perhaps his masterpiece," because "it is nearly impressionist in feeling."[38] Silva doubtless would not have been amused. Nevertheless, Baur's observation is accurate. Its freer handling, greater attention to clouds, and naturalistic light effects render the style far closer to impressionism than most of his earlier works. *A Summer Afternoon* is unusual among Silva's works in this genre because it contains neither the vestiges of a wreck present in *Old and Abandoned* (1883)

[FIG. 28] *Shoreline, Early Evening,* n.d.

nor the threatening rocks of his last dated work *Autumn Afternoon on the New England Coast* (1886, Fig. 34). *A Summer Afternoon,* like *Clearing Off* (c. 1883, Pl. 38), and *Shoreline, Early Evening* (n.d., Fig. 28), does have a threatening mass of clouds hovering at the horizon, however. The low-hanging nimbus clouds appear to sandwich a group of small ships far out at sea between the steely undersides of the clouds and the ominously dark water. Like Martin Johnson Heade's *Thunderstorm over Narragansett Bay* (1868, Fig. 29), the water's color conveys the threat posed by a usually benign force. Of course, Silva dramatically reduced the symbolic dimension of Heade's trope in his composition, veiling it in naturalism. Another aspect of Heade's work, the procession of ships headed for shore in *Thunderstorm* also

surfaces in Silva's late work, particularly *Evening* (Fig. 26). Even as he sought to augment the realism, bordering on impressionism, of his paintings, Silva owed a significant debt to his luminist predecessors. From luminism, he derived the symbolic weight that he felt was so critical in order to prevent a work from slipping into superficial visual trickery, by which he meant impressionism. Appropriately, Heade's significance to Silva became most apparent in the latter's work after he moved to New Jersey, where Heade had worked for many years.

This nuanced application of luminist typology was uncommon, even for Silva. As mentioned above, he was customarily far less circumspect in his application of symbols. Each year the artist was invited to illustrate a work for the American

[FIG. 29] Martin Johnson Heade (1819 – 1904), *Thunderstorm over Narragansett Bay*, 1868, Oil on canvas, 31⅛ x 54¾ inches, Amon Carter Museum, Fort Worth, Texas, Gift of Anne T. and Robert M. Bass

Watercolor Society exhibition catalogue, and he chose to be represented by shipwrecks for three of the last four years of his life.[39] The Society's catalogues were illustrated from ink drawings made by artists after their own works. The drawback of this approach was the loss of color and detail, and Silva fell back on his more overt iconography in order to convey his meaning despite the nature of the medium. As a memento mori, the wreck easily conveyed Silva's meaning to a general audience. Even the lighthouse motif enjoyed a revival in this period, and further reflects the artist's adaptation of his symbols to a particular composition. In both *Holding Her Course* (1883) and *Heading Out* (n.d.), the artist reasserted the lighthouse theme in the context of a vertical composition. By virtue of their shape, lighthouses lend themselves perfectly to this format.

Collectively, these examples suggest that during the 1880s Silva exercised a more complex sense not only of light and color, as seen in his sunsets, but also of typology. As his sense of naturalism flourished, Silva struggled to assert the importance of his luminist iconography in order to preserve his art from deteriorating into impressionist frivolity.

In 1884, Silva finally spoke out against the rise of impressionism in America. The fact that Silva transcribed the "Dandyism" article four years earlier without taking action suggests that he initially felt only a minimal threat from the movement, except as a fad. The proximate cause for Silva's publication of "American vs. Foreign-American Art" was his belief that the younger artists sought to exclude him (and others) from public exhibitions because they did not share the impressionists' "ideas of art." Except for that complaint, Silva's criticism had changed since 1880 only in degree and reiterates the "Dandyism" article almost verbatim. The anonymous author leveled his criticism at the superficiality of "dandy" artists:

> Never, it seems to us, were painters so much devoted to painting the outside of things as they are now. We are dazzled everywhere with tricks of color, fantastic dress, subjects chosen only with reference to their adaptation to the revelation of the special cleverness of those who treat them. . . . Our young men, in a great number of instances, are running after these trick-masters, learning nothing of art in its deeper meanings, but supremely busy with the outside of things, and very trivial things at that. In this devotion to the tricks of art, all earnestness and worthiness of purpose die, and art becomes simply a large and useless field of dandyism.[40]

Silva not only copied down this passage into his sketchbook, but he also later incorporated aspects of it into his own diatribe:

> Many of our artists learn certain artists' tricks and then repeat them continually, with no idea of the deeper meaning of art, but

only of the outside of things, and very trivial things at that. All earnestness of purpose is lost, and with them art becomes a useless field of affectation where their tricks of color and handling are displayed. In choice of subject they have in view only how far it will serve their peculiar tricks.[41]

His mild plagiarism aside, Silva's repetition of the earlier essay suggests consistency during the last years of his life. The following year, he wrote of the successful defense of the Watercolor Society against critics and conservatives. He championed the liberalism of the Society in exhibiting, "the best of every school, from the stiff pre-Raphaelite to the wildest freak of impressionism."[42] A back-handed compliment at best for practitioners of either aesthetic, Silva's assessment nevertheless equated artistic liberalism not with modernism or nationalism, but with tolerance.

The competing camps of liberals and conservatives in the later nineteenth century have consistently been interpreted as corresponding to impressionist and Pre-Raphaelite aesthetics respectively. Silva's articles, however, reposition the debate by casting the impressionists as the conservatives who have imposed their aesthetic standards upon others. He professed bafflement at how "young men, fresh from the liberal atmosphere of the European studios, should bring home such narrow-minded notions."[43]

Returning to the metaphorical language of "progress," Silva called upon "the earnest men, working here among us, casting their lot with us" to "help make the close of the nineteenth century famous in the history of American art."[44] To fulfill their patriotic duties, young artists needed both to treat American subject matter and to use memory as an artistic tool to invest their works with meaning instead of "cold facts." He continued that it was "impossible to paint a large and important work entirely out-of-doors."[45] So much of Silva's work contends with national memory, that on some level he undoubtedly equated the practice of studio composition with the artistic investigation of symbolic and national issues. In his often-cited summary of artistic principles, Silva wrote that "A picture must be more than a skillfully painted canvas;—it must tell something. People do not read books simply because they are well printed and handsomely bound."[46]

Even though both luminists and impressionists shared an interest in surface, their purposes in doing so were different. Luminism investigated the picture plane as a sheer, "egoless" abstraction devoid of visible brushwork, where art and nature collided to explore the transcendent presence of God in nature and art. Impressionist landscapes, by contrast, drew attention to the picture plane by presenting viewers with the material aspect of the paint and an immediate awareness of the artist's

mediating vision. One movement tended toward the universal and the divine, while the other championed the individual artist's virtuosity. Although perhaps a reductive reading of both movements, this description is consistent with Silva's portrayal of "American" and "Foreign-American" camps at the end of his career.

Silva's late works demonstrate that he was not a spectator in the struggle between these two groups. Despite his frustration with the impressionists' conservatism and superficiality, he did not align himself with the "stiff pre-Raphaelite" group either. In the middle of this aesthetic range, Silva positioned his own art as an individual compromise. He strove to define an art form that was more depth than surface, but which equally engaged the viewer with increasing naturalism. He viewed American art as an art "in progress," and therefore still highly experimental. He espoused liberalism and inclusiveness because he believed that American artists had to work together to advance their nation. In his history of the Watercolor Society, he claimed that "Competent judges agree that we have made more progress in our water color art, and show a much better exhibition than they do in England."[47]

For Silva, art remained a contest in which America competed with the other nations of the world, and he believed that victory lay in the gradual improvement of a

[FIG. 30] *Late Afternoon*, n.d.

native idiom. Neither the Pre-Raphaelite (British) nor the impressionist (French) aesthetic alone held the promise of eventual supremacy, so Silva pursued a third way between the two extremes and applied it to American subject matter. His paintings of the 1880s, however, gradually edged toward the proto-impressionist sensibility of *A Summer Afternoon at Long Branch* (1885, Fig. 57) and *Late Afternoon* (n.d., Fig. 30) and suggest a trajectory toward increasingly loose handling that aligned him with so distinguished a figure as Winslow Homer. Indeed, Silva's late treatises on art accurately characterize the trend in the native school of American art of which Homer is generally considered to be the primary exemplar.

Silva's aesthetic split during the early 1880s may well reflect his inability to reconcile the two aesthetic modes that had preoccupied him throughout his career. Comparing *Schooner Passing Castle Island* (1874, Fig. 10, Pl. 21) and *Schooner "Progress"* (1875, Fig. 18, Pl. 23) offers a similar dilemma to the one Silva confronted in the early 1880s. Whether or not *Clearing Off* (c. 1883, Pl. 38) and *A Summer Afternoon at Long Branch* (1885, Fig. 57) constituted the beginnings of a new direction for his art is impossible to say because his production was cut short by his early death. Silva's writings do outline a liberal, if profoundly nationalist, vision for American art. The adversarial, argumentative character for which Silva became known during the course of his life in no way impaired his faith in the artistic potential of his country and countrymen.

Patronage & Criticism

The critics never thought much of Silva's work. If not for the patronage of fellow veterans early in his career and the notice taken of his work by prominent collectors in the later 1870s, he might not have survived as an artist at all. Only in the 1880s did Silva garner more attention from the critics, particularly S. G. W. Benjamin, and he may have been better off without it. As the critics at last engaged with his work, the prices that the artist asked for his works dipped. Appropriately, his recovery for late twentieth- and early twenty-first-century audiences may also be attributed to the vision of several prominent collectors along with one art historian, John I. H. Baur. Collectors, however, have consistently been Silva's most reliable supporters.

Whether or not Silva would have flourished, given greater attention from the critics, is debatable. His opinionated nature would have insulated him from the nattering nabobs, but perhaps his work might have benefited from a more demanding audience. Whatever hypothetical scenarios we develop, the evidence so far suggests that critical notice of Silva's work came only late in his career, and was almost certainly stimulated not by his rising talent, but by the prestige of his patrons. The critics rarely said a flattering word about Silva's work, and his inclusion in their articles suggests a need to explain his success with patrons, rather than a nascent appreciation of his paintings.

Silva's first known admirers were army colonels, a fact proudly trumpeted in the National Academy of Design's exhibition catalogues. Col. T. W. Clark owned a work entitled *The Beach at Long Branch, N.J.* in 1869 (probably comparable to Fig. 31) and Col. J. S. Crosby had purchased *Moon Rise at Cape Ann* (unlocated) by 1873.[48] The first painting is a light-filled scene of middle-class leisure along the beach in the Long Branch resort community, while the second was probably a more dramatic composition similar to

[FIG. 31] *Beach at Long Branch, New Jersey*, c. 1869

Moonlight, Cape Ann (n.d.). Silva was apparently able to parlay his military connections into patronage for his art. The appeal of these works for veterans of the Civil War is a matter of speculation, but was undoubtedly partly related to their friendship with the artist.

The two predominant subjects of Silva's early work may depict alternative, but related, responses to end of the war: escapism and mourning. Silva's beach scenes from 1869 and 1870 bear a striking similarity to Homer's *Long Branch, New Jersey* (1869) and the remaining fragments of his *Low Tide* (1869). The artists' shared use of the beach and leisure as symbols in the years after the war would similarly turn to disaffection for the artifices of Thorstein Veblen's "leisure class" with the passage of time, but initially suggest recourse from the recent devastation of war. Silva experimented only briefly with such scenes, one of which, *A Summer*

[FIG. 32] *The Building of Race Rock Lighthouse*, 1874

Promenade along the Beach at Coney Island (1870, Pl. 3), is included in the current exhibition. American flags flying along the shore in several of these leisure scenes assert a patriotic dimension to his subject matter that may also have appealed to veterans. In contrast, the steady, enduring rock in *Moonlight, Cape Ann* metaphorically suggests the strength of the nation in the face of adversity, as discussed earlier in this essay.

A commission from another of Silva's early patrons, Francis Hopkinson Smith (1838 – 1915), reiterates and magnifies the interpretation of Silva's lighthouses. Smith, aside from being an artist himself, was an author and engineer. Among his projects was the finance, design, and construction of new lighthouses after the war. *The Building of Race Rock Lighthouse* (1874, Fig. 32) depicts an early phase

of an heroic, five-year construction effort near New London, Connecticut.[49] William DeCosta has offered an excellent historical account of the project:

A half dozen laborers used derricks to set granite foundations. They lived on the Rock, sheltering themselves in a small house of matched boards with provisions of fuel, water and canvas. It was dangerous work, several died in the effort, and nearly all froze to death in December 1876 when storms covered the Rock with ice, dampening their provisions and threatening their shelter. Construction completed by November, 1878, Race Rock Light produced alternate beams of red and white, seen about fourteen nautical miles out at thirty second intervals; it was also equipped with a fog bell giving two blows every twenty seconds, a circular granite pier, landing wharf, and a dwelling tower.[50]

Silva's work depicts the construction project in extraordinary detail. The man-made island itself takes on the appearance of a ship with its derricks resembling masts and supporting ropes echoing the rigging of the small ship tied up in the foreground. Whether or not Smith specifically designed Race Rock Light, he almost certainly commissioned Silva to paint the ambitious project. Silva's final work is arguably his only overtly historical subject, but it invests his other lighthouse scenes with a sense of the intrepid nobility of lighthouses and their keepers. Moreover, the painting demonstrates that at least one of Silva's patrons recognized the heroic aspect of his art.

During the later 1870s, several prominent collectors noticed Silva's work. The arrival of these collectors and increased demand for his work were paralleled by an enormous increase in the prices that Silva asked for his paintings. In the mid-1870s, Silva was asking only about a hundred dollars for each of his oils, but between 1877 and 1879, that number quintupled. He also began asking nearly comparable prices for his watercolors as his practice of that medium came to dominate his art in the early 1880s. John Gellatly, a major early donor to what is now the Smithsonian American Art Museum, was Silva's first documented high-profile client. Gellatly bought *Twilight at Point Judith, Rhode Island* (unlocated) in 1876, and allowed the artist to exhibit the work at the Brooklyn Art Association exhibition in December of that year. This purchase was perhaps one of the best omens for Silva's artistic future, as Gellatly's taste was generally prophetic. Unfortunately, however, Gellatly does not appear to have kept *Twilight* in his collection until the end of his life when he donated much of it to the Smithsonian.

Other famous patrons, like Thomas B. Clarke and Courtlandt Palmer were less public about their ownership of Silva's work. Clarke's collection was dispersed after his death in 1883, however, and the sales catalogue revealed Silva's 1879 *On the Jersey Coast* (unlocated).[51] Palmer owned Silva's *New London Light* (possibly 1878, unlocated). Perhaps the most notable aspect of these collectors' interest in Silva is its apparent lack of uniformity. Whereas twentieth-century appreciation of Silva's painting has favored his Hudson River scenes of the early 1870s, prominent nineteenth-century collectors gravitated toward several different facets of the artist's work.

The critics fell into line behind the prominent collectors, and so too did Silva's only known dealer, Charles M. Kurtz. In addition to representing Silva at several exhibitions in the midwest, Kurtz was also the editor of the *Art Union* in which Silva published his articles. The two corresponded throughout the early 1880s, and several of Silva's letters have been preserved.[52] Their relationship appears to have remained formal in tone, despite several years of acquaintanceship. The artist cannot have been easy to manage during this period, however, as his success of the late 1870s and early 1880s had encouraged him to take on more financial responsibilities than he could easily administer, including his studio in the Tenth Street building. Patronage for his work appears to have diminished during the 1880s. He consistently reduced his prices at the annual exhibitions (with a few notable exceptions), perhaps hoping to sell more pieces, and churned out his less expensive watercolors rather than producing more of the oils for which he asked five hundred dollars. Silva's letters to Kurtz also betray an increasing level of anxiety as the years progressed. Just months before his death, Silva wrote an especially frank note:

> You were very anxious to take some of my pictures with you and quite sanguine of selling them. I have heard nothing from you and cannot learn that they have been mentioned in any newspaper. I wrote you several weeks ago but rec'd [sic] no reply. I gave you the name of Mr. R. Lucas of St. Louis as one likely to buy a picture. You have taken no notice of my letter if you have received it.

> You are aware that besides the outlay of painting a picture, I also answer the expense of frames.

> If this is only to assist in making an exhibition for some one else's profit, I will plainly state that I cannot afford it. . . .

> I object to my pictures going to Boston if unsold in St. Louis, as Boston doesn't buy pictures and I could do something with the pictures in N.Y. Perhaps Mr. Petters can do something.[53]

No material evidence of Kurtz's feelings toward Silva remains. If his lack of reply to Silva's letter may be taken as representative, however, then he certainly did not worry terribly about keeping him happy. The tone of Silva's letter suggests that he was the more dependent of the two.

Of the several critics believed to have taken notice of Silva's work, only S. G. W. Benjamin can be securely identified. Critics often preferred to remain anonymous during the nineteenth century, perhaps hoping to avoid criticism themselves. The earliest appraisal of Silva's work came in 1878 in the pages of the *New York Daily Tribune* in response to an American Watercolor Society exhibition.

> We do not greatly like Mr. F. A. Silva's productions. His no. 75, Gathering Seaweed—

[FIG. 33] *Along the Shore*, n.d.

Coney Island, is very thin and metallic, but in subject it is interesting in every part, and there is much light and air in it. One of the old Dutchmen would, however, have got more light and air still without half the apparent effort Mr. Silva makes, but if we compare his little picture with either of the big ones we have just mentioned, it will be found that he has put far more material in his small square, than Mr. Hopkinson Smith, Mr. Bricher, and Robbins have in theirs.[54]

Although hardly a roaring start, this initial review incorporates an ambivalence that characterized nearly all criticism of his work. The author's notice of Silva's color as "metallic" was especially portentous. In Benjamin's two critiques of the artist's work in 1880 and 1881, he pointed

out "the occasional crudeness of colouring" and a "brassy hue" in one of Silva's watercolors.[55] The 1881 article notes, however, that Silva's work had begun to show "perhaps increased softness of color." When the artist relinquished his brighter palette, he apparently faced some opposition from critics who preferred wider color ranges. Although Silva continued to experiment with color during the 1880s, he did not move assertively in the direction that Benjamin recommended. The steely sky of *Clearing Off* (c. 1883, Pl. 38) suggests instead that Silva stubbornly persisted in his metallic aesthetic.

Of Silva's compositional sense and drawing ability, on the other hand, the critics never wrote an ill word. Benjamin spoke for several of them when he noted that there were "few artists who are so accurate in drawing or so conscientious

[FIG. 34] *Autumn Afternoon on the New England Coast*, 1886

is that Silva did not fall comfortably in to either the impressionist or the Pre-Raphaelite camp. Consequently, journals and critics favoring one aesthetic or the other found flaws in his works that they believed aligned him too closely with the competition. Not surprisingly, such indecisive and transparently biased criticism appears not to have influenced the artist's development greatly during the period. As a consequence, however, he was stung by both sides and failed to garner any significant degree of publicity for himself and his work.

The kindest words published about Silva were written for his obituaries. Isolating the aspects in his work that had most distinguished him, these writers described Silva primarily as an outstanding watercolorist and a talented draftsman who "particularly excelled in the painting of beach and surf."[59] Oddly, those traits correspond with the least remembered aspects of his work today. Silva successfully capitalized upon his military connections in order to get started as a professional artist and from there was able to cultivate more distinguished patrons. During the 1880s, however, he encountered the limitations of going it alone. His opinionated nature and strong sense of independence prevented him from joining a particular aesthetic fraternity after the decline of luminism. Instead, he preferred a more ecumenical approach, stressing an open-mindedness toward all efforts to advance American art. Silva thus prized

in the rendering of detail"[56] as Silva. On this point, however, there was considerable inconsistency, as a *New York Times* critic compared Silva's work to William Trost Richards' in that his paintings were "art with the genius left out, a trial of exactness and industry between the painter and the maker of fine colored photographs. We can respect the labor expended, but ask in vain for an emotion."[57] Those terms are ironically close to the language in which Silva criticized the "stiff" Pre-Raphaelites. Likewise, however, the artist was flogged for his 1885 *A Stormy Day in Narragansett* (unlocated) in which he was "too painty."[58] What these opposed critiques demonstrate more than anything else patriotism above aesthetics, and thereby removed himself from the mainstream of post-bellum American art.

After the war, most American artists rushed to master one of several stylistic modes being imported from abroad, and generally identified themselves with a single school. The question of national artistic identity was largely subsumed by questions of style and modernism, and Silva fell into increasing isolation until the end of his life. Had he lived longer, perhaps Silva could have weathered the storm himself and developed a muscular realism similar to that practiced by Winslow Homer. As it was, Silva was largely forgotten within years of his death, marginalized as a remnant of a native school of landscape and a hold-out against the more cosmopolitan fashions of the 1870s and 1880s.

Conclusion

Silva was unable to reconcile his revived luminist and proto-impressionist aesthetics before his death in 1886. In the attempt, however, he distinguished himself from many of his peers by defying convention and placing patriotism ahead of aestheticism. Even though he could not personally resolve American art's schism, a split that continued to divide American artists well into the twentieth century, Silva decisively condemned superficial aestheticism and struggled

to identify uniquely American subjects with symbolic heft. By reordering the elements of those subjects in his various works within a particular theme, the artist demonstrated a continued faith in the grammar of luminism, if not in its distinctive quality of light. Firmly based in luminism, Silva successfully translated its principles into watercolor, and in that medium arguably showed the most promise for integrating subject, style, and light. In watercolor, he was far less reserved about paint application, and the works often assert themselves with looser brushwork and a lightened palette that set them apart from his late work in oil. Published the year before his death, Silva's article describing the potential of American artists to surpass the world in the medium of watercolor may offer an important clue about the direction he planned to take with his art in the ensuing years.

To the bitter end, Silva showed his national colors. The shipwrecks, lighthouses, storms, and rocky shores that captivated him in the wake of the Civil War continued to dominate his production in the 1880s. Silva's works are rife with such symbolism, and apparently appealed to other veterans in the late 1860s as well. The relevance of the war to Silva's own experience may be inferred from the symbols that he employed and his few writings. As has been argued, his use of symbols, in particular, demonstrates a progression over time away from the transcendent, divine aspect of landscape toward a more human dimension. Although not without exceptions, this trend implies a degree of hope for the future. As lighthouses proliferated along the American coastline, they suggest the possibility of prevention and deterrence. The deadly wrath of nature in the form of storms could increasingly be averted by the technological enhancements and construction of new lighthouses. Silva never included the victims of the shipwrecks that he painted. Instead he anthropomorphized the wrecks themselves, rendering them surrogates for the fatalities. As time wore on, even these surrogates evolved, and they appear less as intact, recognizable remains than almost prehistoric fossils partially submerged in the sands of time. Silva's relationship to war and country also defined his relationship to the American seascape; as time distanced him from the events of the war, his memory, an element that he described as essential to art, likewise altered his depictions of the shore.

Silva's art finally represents an end and a beginning in American art. The Civil War is generally acknowledged by historians to have been a watershed in the nation's cultural development. The nation wrought by war in many ways did not resemble the one that the artist had known before it. As the north turned sharply toward industrialization and southerners struggled to rebuild in defeat, artists too had to adjust. Silva's commitment to art in the wake of the war suggests a need to use it as a medium to contend with recent events. The memory of the halcyon era before the war is represented in his art by the *Progress*, a once proud, white hull cast up on shore and shattered by the storm. For Silva, as for many Americans, the war brutally divided memory into before and after. In his own career, painting the *Progress* offered a similar turning point as the artist shifted increasingly from the ante-bellum luminist idiom to experiment with new aesthetic modes. Although Silva's later work does not fall comfortably under the aegis of any currently identified style, it signaled a discontentment with earlier forms that characterized American art of the period. There he was in the majority.

Notes

1. Unsigned manuscript dated 9 July 1867, photocopy in John I. H. Baur Papers, Box 8, Archives of American Art, Smithsonian Institution, Washington, D.C..

2. William DeCosta, "F. A. Silva: Painter of the Shore" (unpublished typescript, William DeCosta Papers, Archives of American Art, Smithsonian Institution, Washington, D.C., 1975), 1. Baur has observed that he could not substantiate DeCosta's claim, and therefore doubted its accuracy. John I. H. Baur, "Francis A. Silva, Beyond Luminism," *The Magazine Antiques* 118.5 (November 1980), n. 19, 1031. DeCosta, however, has proven to be a highly reliable source, and there is no evidence to refute his claim. George Groce and David Wallace also corroborate DeCosta's account. George C. Groce and David H. Wallace, *The New-York Historical Society's Dictionary of Artists in America, 1564 – 1860* (New Haven and London: Yale University Press, 1957), s.v. "Silva, Francis A.".

3. Undated obituary presumed to be from a New York publication, photocopy in Baur Papers.

4. *Trow's New York City Directory* (1859), 782. Silva continued to list himself for the succeeding two years in *Wilson's Business Directory* under the heading "Painters, House & Sign." Listing himself separately from his master suggests that he was no longer an apprentice.

5. Francis A. Silva to Major General Hunter, 1 April 1863, in Military File of Francis A. Silva, Old Military Records, Military Archives Division, National Archives and Records Service, Washington, D.C.; photocopy in DeCosta Papers.

6. Both Dave's written permission for leave and the record of Silva's reinstatement are contained in his military file in Washington and are included in photocopy form in the DeCosta Papers. Baur has suggested that Silva's illness was, in fact, malaria, a common affliction among troops operating in Virginia. Baur, 1022.

7. Jervis McEntee, Diary, 3 April 1886, microfilm reel D-180, frame 625, Archives of American Art, Smithsonian Institution, Washington, D.C..

8. This was the same regiment that Gifford joined in 1861. There is no evidence that the two men knew one another at the time, but they were in the regiment together for several months before Silva's promotion.

9. Nicolai Cikovsky, Jr. and Franklin Kelly, *Winslow Homer*, exh. cat. (Washington, D.C.: National Gallery of Art; New Haven and London: Yale University Press, 1995), 42.

10. In 1877, McEntee recorded that Col. Hawkins received a letter from Silva, relaying news of the death of portraitist Jacob Blondel (1817 – 1877). McEntee, Diary, 8 May 1877. Silva apparently transferred to Hawkins' company after serving briefly with Duryea's Zouaves in the Fifth New York Regiment according to his 1863 letter to Major General Hunter.

11. Baur, 1022. DeCosta, "F. A. Silva," 2. Charles Jolly Werner, "F. A. Silva" (unpublished manuscript, Charles Jolly Werner Papers, New-York Historical Society, New York, c. 1949), 1. Werner is cited only rarely in this essay because his brief biographical sketch of Silva is riddled with errors.

12. DeCosta, "F. A. Silva," 2.

13. Baur, 1025. Baur based his theory upon a few loosely dated sketches in the Peabody Essex and archival sources, none of which has either a specific date or location. Identification of the sketches was made solely upon the type of boats portrayed. A substantially more likely hypothesis is that Silva copied some of the many paintings of Venetian subjects then on display in New York. The Peabody Essex has dated sketches from May through December of 1879, all of which appear to be American subjects and some of

which are specifically described as scenes of New Jersey. Silva also attended a meeting of the American Watercolor Society in New York on 19 November 1879. American Watercolor Society, "Minutes," 19 November 1879, 153 (Archives of American Art, Smithsonian Institution, Washington, D.C., microfilm reel N68-8). If Silva did go to Venice in 1879, it was one of the shortest, least productive trips of his life. The evidence from 1883 is equally convincing, as Silva completed dated sketches of New York area subjects from March through November.

14. "Secondary Proof of Marriage [of Maggie A. Watts and Francis A. Silva]," 28 March 1893, photocopy, DeCosta Papers.

15. Francis A. Silva, "American vs. Foreign-American Art," *The Art-Union* 1 (June – July 1884), 130 – 31.

16. Ibid., 130.

17. Bureau of Records, Health Department of the City of New York, "A Transcript from the Record of Deaths in the City of New York," 16 January 1893; photocopy in DeCosta Papers.

18. Undated obituary, see note 3.

19. Anonymous, "A Well Known Painter Dead," *New York Herald*, 1 April 1886, 10.

20. McEntee, Diary, 3 April 1886.

21. John Wilmerding, *Fitz Hugh Lane* (New York, Washington, and London: Praeger Publishers, 1971), 89.

22. Barbara Novak, "On Defining Luminism," in John Wilmerding, *American Light: The Luminist Movement, 1850 – 1875*, exh. cat. (Washington, D.C.: National Gallery of Art, 1980), 23 – 30.

23. Ibid., 25.

24. Wayne Craven, "Francis A. Silva (1835 – 86), *Sunrise: Marine View*," in Paul D. Schweizer, ed., *Masterworks of American Art from the Munson Williams Proctor Institute* (New York: Harry N. Abrams, Inc., 1989), 73.

25. Weston Naef, "'New Eyes'—Luminism and Photography," in Wilmerding, *American Light*, 266 – 89.

26. *Approaching Storm* has erroneously been dated c. 1865 in the past. The subject is clearly the *Progress*, and the style is quite close to that of the dated *Schooner "Progress,"* so the work most likely dates from c. 1875.

27. David C. Miller, "The Iconology of Wrecked or Stranded Boats in Mid to Late Nineteenth-Century American Culture," in David C. Miller, ed., *American Iconology, New Approaches to Nineteenth-Century Art and Literature* (New Haven and London: Yale University Press, 1993), 186 – 208 passim.

28. Ibid., 188.

29. Ibid., 198.

30. The Society's Minutes, a brief, unpublished history of the Society by Frank Gervassi, and original copies of several of the Society's exhibition catalogues are located in the Archives of American Art, Smithsonian Institution, Washington D.C. as the "American Watercolor Society Records." Microfilm copies of all of the catalogues are available in the Art Division, New York Public Library.

31. Silva, "American vs. Foreign-American Art," 130.

32. Margaretta M. Lovell, *A Visitable Past: Views of Venice by American Artists, 1860 –* 1915 (Chicago and London: University of Chicago Press, 1989), 8, 38.

33. Ibid., 38.

34. Percy Bysshe Shelley, "Ozymandias," in X. J. Kennedy, *An Introduction to Poetry*, 7th ed. (New York: HarperCollins, 1990), 260, ll. 10 – 14. Lovell, 102.

35. The parallel between the hubris of Ozymandias and the ante-bellum American conception of Progress is certainly appropriate in the current discussion. Silva, like Shelley, describes the inevitable fall of such false idols, when in the Christian tradition there is only one "king of kings." I am grateful to Elizabeth Moodey for pointing out this similarity.

36. Artists were, of course, also attracted to the city by its famous light. Silva never traveled to Venice, but painted at least two finished oils of it anyway, his only foreign subject aside from an imagined tropical sketch in the Peabody Essex collection. Silva's engagement with the city can only superficially be explained by an interest in light that he had never experienced. The subject's attraction for the artist more likely stemmed from its deeper cultural meaning to Americans after the end of the war.

37. Anonymous, "Topics of the Time. Dandyism.," *Scribner's Monthly Illustrated Magazine* 20 (Sept. 1880), 788 – 89. Cited by Silva in his sketchbook in the Peabody Essex collection, acc. no. M8871, book 6, p. 166.

38. Baur, 1029.

39. The works in question were *Long Branch* (1882, no. 147), *A Summer Day on the Coast* (1883, no. 436), and *Point Judith* (1884, no. 636).

40. Anonymous, "Topics of the Time. Dandyism.," 788.

41. Silva, "American vs. Foreign-American Art," 130 – 31.

42. Francis A. Silva, "Our Art Clubs. II.— The American Water Color Society.," *The Art-Union* 2.3 (1885), 52.

43. Silva, "American vs. Foreign-American Art," 130.

44. Ibid., 131.

45. Ibid., 130.

46. Ibid.

47. Silva, "Our Art Clubs," 52.

48. Maria Naylor, compiler, *National Academy of Design Exhibition Record, 1861 – 1900* (New York: Kennedy Galleries, 1973), 2:858. *The Beach at Long Branch* is almost certainly the larger of the two compositions by this title included in the accompanying catalogue of known works as "circa 1869." Although undated, the larger work is inscribed on the back with the title, artist's name, and the same address that Silva listed in the 1868 and 1869 exhibition catalogues: 470 Broadway.

49. A photograph of the painting is in the DeCosta Papers at the Archives of American Art, Smithsonian Institution, Washington, D.C.. The actual painting is currently unlocated.

50. DeCosta, "F. A. Silva," 3.

51. H. Barbara Weinberg, "Thomas B. Clarke: Foremost Patron of American Art, 1872 – 1899," *American Art Journal* 8.1 (May 1976), 80.

52. Charles M. Kurtz Papers, Archives of American Art, Smithsonian Institution, Washington, D.C..

53. Silva to Kurtz, 21 November 1885, Kurtz Papers.

54. Anonymous, "Water Color Society. The Exhibition at the Academy. Public Taste Improving—The Pictures.," *New York Daily Tribune*, 5 February 1878, 5.

55. Samuel Greene Wheeler Benjamin, "American Water-Colour Society. Thirteenth Annual Exhibition," *Art Journal* 6.3 (1880), 91; idem, "V. Fourteenth Annual Exhibition of the American Water Color Society. (Opened January 24. Closed February 23)," *American Art Review* 2.5 (1881), 198.

56. Ibid., "American Water-Colour Society," 91.

57. Anonymous, "More Pictures at the Academy," *New York Times*, 20 April 1884, 6.

58. Anonymous, "The American Water-Color Society Exhibition," *Art Amateur* 12.4 (1885), 81.

59. Anonymous, "A Well Known Painter Dead," 10.

Plates

[PRECEEDING PAGES]
View near New London, Connecticut, 1877 (detail)

PLATE I. *Along the Coast,* 1864   67

PLATE 2. *Off City Island, New York*, 1870

PLATE 4. *Two Unidentified Coasting Vessels*, C. 1870

PLATE 5. *Approaching Storm*, 1871   71

PLATE 6. *Evening in Gloucester Harbor*, 1871

PLATE 7. *Late Afternoon, Haverstraw Bay*, 1871   73

74   PLATE 8. *Moonrise over New York Harbor,* 1871

PLATE 9. *On the Hudson, Nyack,* 1871 75

PLATE 10. *Sunrise, Boston Harbor,* 1871

PLATE II. *Sunset View off the Coast*, 1871　77

PLATE 12. *Ten Pound Island, Gloucester*, 1871–1872

PLATE 13. *Indian Rock, Narragansett Bay,* 1872 79

PLATE 14. *On the Hudson near Haverstraw,* 1872

PLATE 15. *Seining on the Tappan Zee, Nyack, New York,* 1872

81

PLATE 16. *October on the Hudson*, C. 1873

PLATE 17. *Sunrise: Marine View*, c. 1873   83

PLATE 18. *View on the Hudson*, C. 1873

PLATE 19. *Coastal Schooners—Moonrise*, 1874   85

PLATE 20. *Coastal Sunset*, 1874

PLATE 21. *Schooner Passing Castle Island, Boston Harbor,* 1874   87

PLATE 22. *Sunrise at Tappan Zee*, 1874

PLATE 23. *The Schooner "Progress" Wrecked at Coney Island, July 4, 1874, 1875*   89

PLATE 24. *Sunrise at Barnegat Beach, New Jersey*, 1875

PLATE 25. *An August Morning*, 1876

PLATE 26. *The Hudson at Tappan Zee, 1876*

PLATE 27. *View on the Hudson River*, 1876

PLATE 28. *Harbor Scene*, 1877

PLATE 29. *View near New London, Connecticut,* 1877

PLATE 30. *On the North River,* 1879

PLATE 31. *A September Day on the Coast*, 1879   97

PLATE 32. *Along the Connecticut Shore*, 1880

PLATE 33. *Low Tide*, 1880

PLATE 34. *Marsh Scene*, 1880

PLATE 35. *A Summer Day on the Coast*, 1882   101

PLATE 36. *Boats at Anchor*, 1883

PLATE 37. *Cape Elizabeth, Maine*, 1883   103

PLATE 38. *Clearing Off,* C. 1883

PLATE 39. *Off Rockaway Beach*, 1883   105

PLATE 40. *Off the Coast*, 1883

PLATE 41. *Shore Scene*, 1883   107

PLATE 42. *Hudson River at Kingston Point*, n.d.

PLATE 43. *On the Hudson River, Nyack,* n.d.   109

PLATE 44. *Palisades of the Hudson River*, n.d.

PLATE 45. *Robin's Reef Lighthouse off Tomkinsville, New York Harbor*, n.d.

PLATE 46. *Schooner on a River*, n.d.

PLATE 47. *Seascape with Sailboats,* n.d.   113

Sketches from the Collection of the Peabody Essex Museum

PLATE 48. *Town Skyline at Sunset*, September 25, 1867 (Acc. No. 125248.47)   115
PLATE 49. *Noonday* (recto), October 1, 1869 (Acc. No. M8871-F3.6)

116   PLATE 50. *Bass Rocks*, September 5, 1871 (Acc. No. M8871-B1.3)

             PLATE 51. *Schooner Lula Newton, Fisher's Island*, October 4, 1873 (Acc. No. 123351C.2)

PLATE 52. *Rockaway, Long Island,* June 25, 1876 (Acc. No. 123351c.20)   117

At Seabright – Octo 10 – 82 –

PLATE 53. *At Seabright*, October 10, 1882 (Acc. No. 125248.29)

PLATE 54. *Causeway* (recto), n.d. (Acc. No. 125248.14)

PLATE 55. *Baker's Island Light*, July 31, n.y. (Acc. No. 123351B.13)

PLATE 56. *Pigeon Cove*, August 31, n.y. (Acc. No. M8871-F4.1)
PLATE 57. *Sunset Study*, n.d. (Acc. No. 125248.2)

PLATE 58. *Various Vessels*, n.d. (Acc. No. M8871-F2.2)

Catalogue of Known Works
by Francis A. Silva

Mark D. Mitchell

The following catalogue represents a compilation of Silva's artworks known from a variety of sources, including auction records, magazine advertisements, exhibition catalogues, archives, curatorial research files, library records, private gallery records, and on-line databases. Like any preliminary inventory, however, the list undoubtedly contains some errors, oversights, and a degree of redundancy. Secondary sources such as gallery advertisements and auction records have been relied upon for object descriptions and may be in error. In several cases, basic information about paintings is missing or contradicted by different records. Such situations often arose when a secondary source was copied for a museum's or gallery's research file, for example, but did not include a complete description or offer a bibliographic citation to pursue.

Silva's works are divided under three headings: dated paintings, undated paintings, and a brief summary of the collection at the Peabody Essex Museum in Salem, Massachusetts. The Peabody Essex has by far the most substantial holdings of preparatory sketches and studies by the artist in a single collec-tion. As Silva's work becomes better known to scholars and the public, the museum's collection will offer a bounty of new research avenues to explore.

A note with regard to the categories into which the works are organized: almost no effort has been made to revise previous descriptions or attributions. In only a few egregious cases have corrections been made, and those are generally explained in brackets within the individual entries. Where several different titles have been used for a single work, the most recent will be cited, followed by earlier permutations in parentheses. The listing includes over two hundred of the artist's known works in oil and watercolor that are believed to be finished compositions. With the exception or the Peabody Essex's collection, preparatory works have been excluded from the catalogue as a practical consideration. Paintings "attributed" to Silva have also been omitted.

Note that works illustrated within the following checklist immediately precede their catalogue entries. Figure and plate numbers for all illustrated works (including those shown in the essays) are also listed.

[LEFT] *Low Tide*, 1880 (detail)

1. Dated Paintings

1864

Along the Coast
[FIG. I, page II; PL. I, page 67]
Watercolor on paper, 11½ x 17⅝ in.
Signed and dated, l.r.
PROVENANCE
Private Collection, MA (current)

1869

An August Morning at Cohasset, Massachusetts
Oil on canvas, 18 x 36 in.
Signed and dated, l.l.
PROVENANCE
Private Collection, NY (current)
Hollis Taggart Galleries, NY (2001)

Beach at Long Branch, New Jersey
[circa 1869]
[FIG. 31, page 53]
Oil, 8 x 16 in.
Signed
Photograph © Christie's Images, New York 2002
PROVENANCE
Christie's, NY (1992)
Sotheby's, NY (1989)

The Beach at Long Branch, New Jersey [circa 1869]
Oil on canvas, 12 x 24 in.
Signed, l.r.
PROVENANCE
Sotheby's, NY (1984)

1870

Approaching Storm
Oil on canvas, 14 x 12 in.
Signed and dated, l.l.
PROVENANCE
Sotheby's, NY (1991)

[FIG. 35]
Cape Ann (Sundown, Summer Seascape, Cape Ann, Mass.)
Oil on canvas, 20½ x 40 in.
Signed and dated, l.l.
Photograph courtesy of Sotheby's, Inc. ©2002

PROVENANCE
Sotheby's, NY (2000)
Private Collection, PA
Christie's, NY (1979)
Donald Purdy, CT
Coe Kerr Gallery, NY (1978)
Kennedy Galleries, NY (1970)
Vose Galleries, MA
LITERATURE
Baur, 1980, fig. 2, p. 1020.
William H. Gerdts, *American Luminism*, exh. cat. (New York: Coe Kerr Gallery, 1978), no. 32. [Width differs; apparently an error as work is identical]
EXHIBITED
Coe Kerr Gallery, NY, "American Luminism," 1978.

The New England Coast [circa 1870]
Oil on canvas, 20 x 40 in.
Signed, l.r.
PROVENANCE
William Vareika Fine Arts, RI (1995)

Off City Island, New York
[FIG. 12, page 28; PL. 2, page 68]
Oil on canvas, 20¼ x 40¼ in.
Signed and dated, l.r.
PROVENANCE
New-York Historical Society, NY,
1975.22 (current)
Hirschl & Adler Galleries, NY (1975)
Palm Beach Galleries, FL (1974)
LITERATURE
Richard J. Koke, compiler, *American
Landscape and Genre Paintings in the
New-York Historical Society: A Catalogue
of the Collection, Including Historical,
Narrative, and Marine Art* (New York:
New-York Historical Society, 1982),
vol. III, no. 2470, p. 139. [Mistakenly
dated 1878.]
Palm Beach Galleries, *19th and 20th
Century French and American Paintings*,
exh. cat. (Palm Beach, Florida:
Palm Beach Galleries, 1974), no. 32.
EXHIBITED
Palm Beach Galleries, Palm Beach, FL,
"19th and 20th Century French and
American Paintings," 1974.

Off the Gloucester Coast [circa 1870]
Oil on canvas, 9 x 18 in.
Signed, l.l.
PROVENANCE
R. R. R. Associates, NH (1975)

Sailing on the Hudson [circa 1870]
Oil on canvas, 11½ x 23½ in.
Signed, l.r.
PROVENANCE
D. Wigmore Fine Art, NY (1998)
S. Dean Levy, NY (1967)

**A Summer Promenade along the
Beach at Coney Island**
[PL. 3, page 69]
Oil on canvas, 6¼ x 16 in.
Signed and dated with location, l.l.
PROVENANCE
Private Collection, IL (current)
Hirschl & Adler Galleries, NY (1982)

Sunrise on the Coast of Maine
Oil on canvas, 20 x 40 in.
Signed and dated, l.r.
PROVENANCE
Richard A. Bourne Co., MA (1974)

**Two Unidentified Coasting Vessels
(Two Coasters and a Half Brig
in Boston Bay; Waiting for Wind
and Tide)** [circa 1870]
[PL. 4, page 70]
Oil on canvas, 23½ x 39½ in.
Signed, l.l.
PROVENANCE
Peabody Essex Museum, MA (current)
Charles Henry Cooper (1956)
LITERATURE
M. V. and Dorothy Brewington, *The
Marine Paintings and Drawings in the
Peabody Museum* (Salem, Mass.: Peabody
Museum, 1968), no. 1311, p. 334.

View from the Hudson River
Oil, 9 x 18 in.
Dated
PROVENANCE
Butterfields, CA (1993)

1871

Approaching Storm
[PL. 5, page 71]
Oil on canvas, 12 x 24 in.
Signed and dated, l.l.
PROVENANCE
Private Collection, MA (current)
Sotheby's, NY (1993)

Coast of Maine
Oil on canvas, 10 x 18 in.
Signed and dated, l.r.
PROVENANCE
Sotheby's, NY (1989)
Mrs. Walter H. Rubin

Evening in Gloucester Harbor
[PL. 6, page 72]
Oil on canvas, 20 x 40 in.
Signed and dated, l.l.
PROVENANCE
Private Collection, WA (current)
Christie's, NY (1999)

[FIG. 36]

Gloucester Fishing Fleet
Oil, 9 x 18 in.
Signed and dated
Photograph © Christie's Images, New York 2002

PROVENANCE
Christie's, NY (1993)

Gray Day at Cape Ann
Oil on canvas, 9 x 19 in.
Signed

PROVENANCE
Florence Katz, NJ (1993)

The Hudson River Looking toward the Catskills
[FIG. 17, page 33]
Oil on canvas, 20 x 40⅛ in.
Signed and dated, l.l.

PROVENANCE
Private Collection, DC (current)
Christie's, NY (2001)
William Hutton
The Old Print Shop, NY (1957)

EXHIBITED
Williams College Museum of Art,
Williamstown, MA, extended loan,
1968–71.

Late Afternoon, Haverstraw Bay
[PL. 7, page 73]
Oil on canvas, 20 x 36 in.
Signed, l.r.

PROVENANCE
A. J. Kollar Fine Paintings, WA (1998)
Christie's, NY (1994)
Sotheby's, NY (1981

Moonrise over New York Harbor
[PL. 8, page 74]
Oil on canvas, 11½ x 17½ in.
Signed, l.r.

PROVENANCE
Private Collection, VA (1983)
Richard York Gallery, NY (as representative, 1983)
Hirschl & Adler Galleries, NY (1983)
Richard Manoogian, MI
Jeffrey R. Brown, MA (1982)
Charles E. Buckley, NH (1980)
Vose Galleries, MA

On the Hudson, Nyack
[PL. 9, page 75]
Oil on canvas, 11½ x 23½ in.
Signed and dated, l.l.

PROVENANCE
Private Collection, MA (current)
Paul A. Kossey (1980)
Childs Gallery, MA (1970)

LITERATURE
John K. Howat, ed., *American Paradise: The World of the Hudson River School*, exh. cat. (New York: Metropolitan Museum of Art, 1987), pp. 317–18.
Baur, 1980, pl. 1, p. 1019.

Sailing at Sunset (Red Sails at Sunset)
Oil on canvas, 15 x 30 in.
Signed and dated, l.r.

PROVENANCE
Hirschl & Adler Galleries, NY (1978)

LITERATURE
Hirschl & Adler Galleries, *The American Scene: A Survey of the Life and Landscape of the 19th Century*, exh. cat. (New York: Hirschl & Adler Galleries, 1969), no. 79, p. 65.

EXHIBITED
Hirschl & Adler Galleries, NY, "The American Scene: A Survey of the Life and Landscape of the 19th Century," 1969.

[FIG. 37]

Ships Becalmed
Oil on canvas, 12 x 24 in.
Signed and dated
Photograph courtesy of Sotheby's, Inc. ©2002

PROVENANCE
Sotheby's, NY (1998)

Sunrise, Boston Harbor
[PL. 10, page 76]
Oil on canvas, 12 x 24 in.
Signed and dated, l.r.
PROVENANCE
Private Collection, CA (current)
Godel & Co., Inc., NY (1994)
Private Collection, MA
Vose Galleries, MA

Sunset View off the Coast
[PL. 11, page 77]
Oil on canvas, 12¼ x 24¼ in.
Signed and dated, l.l.
PROVENANCE
Private Collection, MA (current)

Ten Pound Island, Gloucester [1871–72]
[PL. 12, page 78]
Oil on canvas, 14⅛ x 24¼ in.
Signed, l.l.
PROVENANCE
Terra Museum of American Art, IL,
Daniel J. Terra Collection, 1999.137
(current)

Wreck of the Mary Anna
Oil on canvas, 20 x 40 in.
PROVENANCE
Childs Gallery, MA (1986)

1872

Boston Harbor
Oil on canvas, 15 x 30 in.
Signed and dated, l.l.
PROVENANCE
Henry S. Streeter (1980)
LITERATURE
Baur, 1980, fig. 4, p. 1021.

[FIG. 38]
Cuttyhunk Light
Oil on canvas, 20 x 36 in.
Signed and dated, l.l.
PROVENANCE
Vallejo Maritime Gallery, CA

Indian Rock, Narragansett Bay
[FIG. 2, page 12; PL. 13, page 79]
Oil on canvas, 20 x 36 in.
Signed and dated, l.r.
PROVENANCE
Mr. and Mrs. Erving Wolf, TX (current)
Sotheby's, NY (1977)
LITERATURE
Baur, 1980, fig. 5, p. 1022 [misidentified
as Brace's Rock, Cape Ann].
John Wilmerding, *American Light:
The Luminist Movement, 1850–1875*, exh.
cat. (New York: Harper & Row;
Washington, DC: National Gallery of
Art, 1980), fig. 145, pp. 130–31.

Moonrise
Oil on canvas, 14 x 24 in.
Signed and dated, l.r.
PROVENANCE
Christie's, NY (1991)

[FIG. 39]
**Old Wreck Near Newport,
Rhode Island** [circa 1872]
Oil on board, 6½ x 12¼ in.
Signed l.l.
Photograph courtesy Vance Jordan Fine Art, Inc.
PROVENANCE
Vance Jordan Fine Art, NY

On the Hudson near Haverstraw
[PL. 14, page 80]
Oil on canvas, 18¼ x 30⅜ in.
Signed and dated, l.l.
PROVENANCE
Terra Museum of American Art,
IL, Daniel J. Terra Collection,
1993.16 (current)
Sotheby's, NY (1993)

[FIG. 40]

Sailing Vessels off Cape Ann
Oil on canvas, 14 x 24⅛ in.
Signed and dated, l.l.
Photograph © Christie's Images, New York 2002

PROVENANCE
Christie's, NY (1991)

Seining on the Tappan Zee, Nyack, New York (The Hudson River from the Tappan Zee)
[PL. 15, page 81]
Oil on canvas, 20¼ x 36 in.
Signed and dated, l.l.
Photograph courtesy Richard York Gallery, NY

PROVENANCE
Richard York Gallery, NY (1987)
Vose Galleries, MA (1985)
Anderson Galleries, NY (1984)
Anderson Galleries, NY (1938)
Robert Fridenberg, NY (1938)

1873

[FIG. 41]

Calm at Sunset
Oil on canvas, 29 x 50 in.
Signed and dated, l.r.
Photograph courtesy of Sotheby's, Inc. © 2002

PROVENANCE
Sotheby's, NY (1993)

Calm Sunset
[FIG. 13, page 30]
Oil on canvas, 20 x 36 in.
Signed and dated, l.l.
Photograph © Christie's Images, New York 2002

PROVENANCE
Christie's, NY (1986)

Kingston Point, Hudson River
[circa 1873]
Oil on canvas, 20 x 36 in.
Signed, l.r.

PROVENANCE
Thyssen-Bornemisza Collection, Madrid (current)
Vose Galleries, MA (1984)
Sotheby's, NY (1980)

LITERATURE
Barbara Novak, "Francis A. Silva, 1835–1886, Kingston Point, Hudson River," in Barbara Novak and Elizabeth Garrity Ellis, eds., *The Thyssen-Bornemisza Collection, Nineteenth-Century American Painting* (New York: Sotheby's Publications, 1986), no. 36, pp. 142–43.

October on the Hudson [circa 1873]
[PL. 16, page 82]
Oil on canvas, 24 x 44 in.
Signed, l.l.
Photograph © Christie's Images, New York 2002

PROVENANCE
John and Dolores Beck (current)
Christie's, NY (1993)
Kennedy Galleries, NY (1960)

LITERATURE
Valerie Ann Leeds, "Francis Augustus Silva (1835–1886), October on the Hudson, c. 1873," in Valerie Ann Leeds, *An American Palette: Works from the Collection of John and Dolores Beck*, exh. cat. (St. Petersburg, Florida: Museum of Fine Arts; Orlando, Florida: Orlando Museum of Art, 2001), 106–7.

EXHIBITED
St. Petersburg Museum of Fine Arts and Orlando Museum of Art, FL, "An American Palette: Works from the Collection of John and Dolores Beck," 2001.

River Scene
Oil on canvas, 15 x 30¼ in.
Signed and dated, l.r.

PROVENANCE
Sotheby's, NY (1974)

LITERATURE
Baur, 1980, fig. 6, p. 1023.

Sunrise: Marine View [PL. 17, page 83]

[PL. 17, page 83]

Oil on canvas, 15 x 29⅞ in.

Signed, l.r.

PROVENANCE

Munson Williams Proctor Institute, NY
(current)

Sotheby's, NY (1984)

Sotheby's, NY (1981)

Hirschl & Adler Galleries, NY (1972)

LITERATURE

Wayne Craven, "Francis A. Silva
(1835–1886), Sunrise: Marine View," in
Paul D. Schweizer, ed., *Masterworks of
American Art from the Munson Williams
Proctor Institute* (New York: Harry N.
Abrams, 1989), no. 30, pp. 72–73.

Wayne Craven and Richard Martin,
*Two Hundred Years of American Art.
The Munson Williams Proctor Institute*
(Seattle and London: University of
Washington Press, 1986), no. 25, p. 39.

Baur, 1980, fig. 3, p. 1020.

Hirschl & Adler Galleries, *Faces and
Places: Changing Images of 19th Century
America*, exh. cat. (New York: Hirschl &
Adler Galleries, 1972–73), no. 84.

EXHIBITED

New Jersey State Museum, Trenton, NJ,
"This Land is Your Land," 1976.

Lowe Art Museum, Coral Gables, FL,
"19th Century American Topographic
Painters," 1974–75.

Mint Museum of Art, Charlotte, NC,
"19th Century American Paintings," 1974.

Hirschl & Adler Galleries, NY, "Faces
and Places: Changing Images of 19th
Century America," 1972–73.

Sunrise: Marine View

Oil on canvas, 19½ x 39¾ in.

Signed and dated

PROVENANCE

Private Collection, AZ (1989)

**View on the Hudson (View on
the Hudson, the Catskills in the
Distance)** [circa 1873]

[PL. 18, page 84]

Oil on canvas, 12 x 20 in.

Signed, l.r.

PROVENANCE

Erving and Joyce Wolf, TX (current)

Coe Kerr Gallery, NY (1980)

Mrs. Norman B. Woolworth, ME (1970)

LITERATURE

Barbara Novak, "Francis A. Silva,
1835–1886, Kingston Point, Hudson
River," in Barbara Novak and Elizabeth
Garrity Ellis, eds., *The Thyssen-
Bornemisza Collection, Nineteenth-
Century American Painting* (New York:
Sotheby's Publications, 1986), p. 142.

Baur, 1980, fig. 7, p. 1023.

William H. Gerdts, *American Luminism*,
exh. cat. (New York: Coe Kerr Gallery,
1978), fig. 31.

Coe Kerr Gallery, *The American
Paintings Collection of Mrs. N. B.
Woolworth*, exh. cat. (New York: Coe
Kerr Gallery, 1970), p. 60.

EXHIBITED

Coe Kerr Gallery, NY, "American
Luminism," 1978.

Coe Kerr Gallery, NY, "The American
Paintings Collection of Mrs. N. B.
Woolworth," 1970.

1874

**The Building of Race Rock Lighthouse
(Race Rock Lighthouse)**

[FIG. 32, page 54]

Oil on canvas, 20 x 37 in.

Signed and dated, l.l.

Photograph courtesy Kennedy Galleries, NY

PROVENANCE

Kennedy Galleries, NY (1977)

Buoy 9

Oil on canvas, 10 x 14 in.

Signed and dated, l.r.

PROVENANCE

Barridoff, ME (1984)

Coastal Schooners – Moonrise

[PL. 19, page 85]

Oil on canvas, 13½ x 23½ in.

Signed and dated, l.l.

PROVENANCE

Lawrence and Jennifer Goichman, CT
(current)

Coastal Sunset (Seascape at Sunset)

[PL. 20, page 86]

Oil on canvas, 14 x 26 in.

Signed and dated, l.r.

PROVENANCE

Private Collection, NY (current)

Sotheby's, NY (1989)

Alexander Gallery, NY (1988)

Sotheby's, NY (1988)

LITERATURE

David C. Miller, ed., *American Iconology*
(New Haven: Yale University Press,
1993), fig. 9.2, pp. 186–87.

Ferryboats near the Battery (Ferry Boats near the Battery at Sunset)
[FIG. 16, page 32]
Oil on canvas, 12 x 20 in.
Signed and dated, l.l.
Photograph courtesy Kennedy Galleries, NY

PROVENANCE
Kennedy Galleries, NY

Schooner Passing Castle Island, Boston Harbor
[FIG. 10, page 26; PL. 21, page 87]
Oil on canvas, 22 x 38 in.
Signed and dated, l.l.

PROVENANCE
The Bostonian Society, Old State House, Boston, MA (current)

LITERATURE
John Wilmerding, *American Marine Painting* (2nd ed., New York: Henry N. Abrams, 1987), fig. 141, pp. 55, 145.
John Wilmerding, *American Light: The Luminist Movement, 1850–1875*, exh. cat. (New York: Harper & Row; Washington, D.C.: National Gallery of Art, 1980), pl. 23, fig. 347, p. 306.
Thomas Wendell Parker, "Topographical and Marine Paintings in the Bostonian Society," *The Magazine Antiques* (March 1979), pl. 10, p. 531.

Sunrise at Tappan Zee (Sunrise)
[PL. 22, page 88]
Oil on canvas, 20 1/16 x 36 1/8 in.
Signed and dated, l.r.

PROVENANCE
Jo Ann and Julian Ganz, Jr., CA (current)
Hirschl & Adler Galleries, NY (1975)
William Schaus, NY

LITERATURE
John Wilmerding, "An American Perspective: Nineteenth-Century Art from the Collection of Jo Ann and Julian Ganz, Jr.," *The Magazine Antiques* (January 1982), pl. 5, p. 261.
Baur, 1980, fig. 8, p. 1024.

EXHIBITED
National Gallery of Art, Washington, DC, "An American Perspective: Nineteenth-Century Art from the Collection of Jo Ann and Julian Ganz, Jr.," 1982.
Los Angeles County Museum of Art, CA, "Pertaining to the Sea," 1976.

1875

America's Cup Race [1875–76]
Oil on canvas, 31 x 48 in.
Signed and dated, l.l.

PROVENANCE
Christie's, NY (1986)
Christie's, NY (1984)

Approaching Storm [circa 1875]
Oil on canvas, 20 x 38 in.
Signed, l.l.

PROVENANCE
Childs Gallery, MA (1972)

Beach and Sea
Oil on canvas, 12 x 20 in.
Signed and dated, l.l.

PROVENANCE
Hirschl & Adler Galleries, NY (1978)

Dunes
[FIG. 22, page 40]
Oil on canvas, 10 1/2 x 30 in.
Signed and dated, l.l.

PROVENANCE
Private Collection, NY (current)
Berry-Hill Galleries, NY
Christie's, NY (1996)

October on the Hudson
Oil on canvas, 20 x 36 in.
Signed and dated, l.r.

PROVENANCE
Kennedy Galleries, NY (1970)
Marine Arts Company, MA (1970)

Off Newport, Rhode Island
[FIG. 4, page 14]
Oil on canvas, 14 x 24 in.
Signed and dated, l.l.
Photograph courtesy of Sotheby's, Inc. ©2002

PROVENANCE
Sotheby's, NY (1997)

Rocky Coastline (New England on the Coast)
Watercolor, 18 x 20 1/2 in.
Signed and dated, l.r.

PROVENANCE
Christie's, NY (1996)

Sailing Vessels off Cape Ann
Oil, 10 1/2 x 18 1/4 in.

PROVENANCE
Adam Weschler & Son, DC (1973)

The Schooner "Progress" Wrecked at Coney Island, July 4, 1874

[FIG. 18, page 35; PL. 23, page 89]
Oil on canvas, 20 x 38¼ in.
Signed and dated, l.l.

PROVENANCE

Richard Manoogian, IL (current)
Sotheby's, NY (1981)
John Gardiner, VA, by descent from
below (1981)
Augustus Floyd

LITERATURE

David C. Miller, ed., *American Iconology*
(New Haven: Yale University Press,
1993), fig. 9.3, pp. 189–90.
Sarah Cash, "Francis Augustus Silva
(1835–1886), The Schooner 'Progress'
Wrecked at Coney Island, July 4th, 1874,
1875," in *National Gallery of Art,
American Paintings from the Manoogian
Collection*, exh. cat. (Washington, DC:
National Gallery of Art, 1989), p. 48.

Seascape

Watercolor, 10¾ x 28 in.
Signed and dated

PROVENANCE

William Doyle Galleries, NY (1995)

Sunrise at Barnegat Beach, New Jersey

[PL. 24, page 90]
Oil on canvas, 13½ x 23¾ in.
Signed and dated, l.l.

PROVENANCE

Private Collection, OH (current)

1876

An August Morning (Sunrise on Lake Michigan)

[PL. 25, page 91]
Watercolor on paper, 13⅛ x 20 in.
Signed and dated, l.l.

PROVENANCE

Amon Carter Museum, TX, Gift of
Anne T. and Robert M. Bass (current)
Hirschl & Adler Galleries, NY (1978)

LITERATURE

Baur, 1980, fig. 12, p. 1026.

[FIG. 42]

Flat Rock, Narragansett

Oil on canvas, 20¼ x 30¼ in.
Signed and dated, l.r.
Photograph courtesy of Sotheby's, Inc. ©2002

PROVENANCE

Sotheby's, NY (1978)
Hirschl & Adler Galleries, NY
Marine Arts Gallery, MA (1975)

LITERATURE

Baur, 1980, fig. 10, p. 1024.

The Hudson at Tappan Zee

[PL. 26, page 92]
Oil on canvas, 24¹⁄₁₆ x 42³⁄₁₆ in.
Signed and dated, l.l.

PROVENANCE

Brooklyn Museum of Art, NY, Dick S.
Ramsay Fund 65.10 (current)

LITERATURE

John K. Howat, ed., *American Paradise:
The World of the Hudson River School*,
exh. cat. (New York: Metropolitan
Museum of Art, 1987), pp. 317–18.
Baur, 1980, fig. 9, p. 1024.
Brooklyn Museum, *The Brooklyn
Museum, American Paintings: A Complete
Illustrated Listing of Works in the
Museum's Collection* (Brooklyn: Brooklyn
Museum of Art, 1979), p. 104.
John K. Howat, *The Hudson River and
Its Painters* (New York: Viking Press,
1972; reprint ed., New York: American
Legacy Press, 1983), fig. 16, p. 139.

[FIG. 43]

Manhattan Beach
Oil on canvas, 30⅛ x 18 in.

PROVENANCE
Currier Gallery of Art, NH, Gift of
Henry Edgell, 1972.19 (current)

LITERATURE
*Currier Gallery of Art Collection
Bulletin 1* (1973), fig. 4, p. 26.

[FIG. 44]

Misty Morning, New York Harbor
[circa 1876]
Oil on canvas, 12¼ x 22 in.
*Photograph courtesy Godel & Co., Inc.
Fine Art, NY*

PROVENANCE
Godel & Co., Inc. Fine Art, NY
(current)
Private Collection, NY

Narragansett Point, Rhode Island
Watercolor, 24 x 30 in.

PROVENANCE
Walter Breen, CA (1976)

Seascape [circa 1876]
Watercolor, dimensions unknown

PROVENANCE
Walter Breen, CA (1976)

Seascape at Sunset
Oil on canvas, 20 x 36 in.
Signed and dated, l.l.

PROVENANCE
Sotheby's, NY (1986)
Liros Gallery, VA (1985)
Dr. Mark Howard, VA

Ships on the Horizon
Oil on canvas, 12 x 24 in.
Signed and dated, l.l.

PROVENANCE
Private Collection, FL (1988)

Sunset at Cape Ann
Oil on canvas, 14 x 12 in.
Signed and dated, l.l.

PROVENANCE
Shannon's Fine Art Auctioneers,
CT (2000)

[FIG. 45]

Sunset, New York Harbor [circa 1876]
Oil on canvas, 9 x 18 in.

PROVENANCE
Avery Galleries, PA (current)
Phillips, NY (2001)
Alexander Galleries, NY

View on the Hudson River
[PL. 27, page 93]
Oil on canvas, 14 x 12 in.
Signed and dated, l.l.

PROVENANCE
Berry-Hill Galleries, NY (current)
Shannon's Fine Art Auctioneers,
CT (2000)

1877

Barnegat Bay, New Jersey [circa 1877]
[FIG. 27, page 47]
Oil on canvas, 12 x 20 in.
Signed, l.r.
Photograph © Christie's Images, New York 2002

PROVENANCE
Hirschl & Adler Galleries, NY (2000)
Christie's, NY (1999)
Cleveland Trust Company, OH (1980)
Hirschl & Adler Galleries, NY (1978)

LITERATURE
Baur, 1980, fig. 14, p. 1027.
Knoedler & Co., *What is American in American Art?*, exh. cat. (New York: Knoedler & Co., 1971), ill. p. 62, p. 35.
Hirschl & Adler Galleries, *The American Scene: A Survey of the Life and Landscape of the 19th Century*, exh. cat. (New York: Hirschl & Adler Galleries, 1969), no. 80, p. 65.
EXHIBITED
Knoedler & Co., NY, "What is American in American Art?" 1971.
 Hirschl & Adler Galleries, NY, "The American Scene: A Survey of the Life and Landscape of the 19th Century," 1969.

[FIG. 46]
Evening on the Coast
Oil, 14 x 24 in.
Signed and dated
Photograph © Christie's Images, New York 2002
PROVENANCE
Christie's, NY (1994)

Harbor Scene (Ships in a Harbor, Sunset)
[PL. 28, page 94]
Oil on canvas, 22 x 36¼ in.
Signed and dated, l.l.
PROVENANCE
Private Collection, MA (current)
Christie's, NY (1993)
Wunderlich & Co., NY (1985)
Dr. Robert Aaronson, CT (1980)
Hirschl & Adler Galleries, NY

Schooners
Medium unknown, 14½ x 12¼ in.
PROVENANCE
Kennedy Galleries, NY

View near New London, Connecticut
[PL. 29, page 95]
Opaque watercolor on paper, 17¾ x 27⅝ in.
Signed and dated, l.l.
PROVENANCE
Brooklyn Museum of Art, NY, Dick S. Ramsay Fund 44.195 (current)
Henry Shaw Newman Gallery, NY (1943)
LITERATURE
Baur, 1980, fig. 14, p. 1027.
Henry Shaw Newman Gallery, *Portfolio* 3 (Sept. 1943), p. 9.

1878

Fishing Boats on Jamaica Bay
[FIG. 21, page 39]
Oil on canvas, 21 x 39½ in.
Signed and dated, l.l.
PROVENANCE
Private Collection, FL (current)
Sotheby's, NY (1994)
EXHIBITED
Museum of the Borough of Brooklyn at Brooklyn College, NY, "From Brooklyn to the Sea: Ships, Seafarers, and New York Harbor," 1985.

1879

After the Equinoctial, off Sandy Hook
Oil on canvas, 26 x 40 in.
Signed, l.r.
PROVENANCE
Sotheby's, NY (1981)

The Fisherman's Home
Watercolor on paper, 17¾ x 27½ in.
Signed and dated, l.r.
PROVENANCE
Wunderlich & Co., NY (1984)
William Doyle Galleries, NY (1983)
EXHIBITED
American Watercolor Society Annual Exhibition, NY, 1879, no. 132.

Great South Bay off Fire Island
[FIG. 23, page 41]
Watercolor on paper, 16 9/16 x 27⅜ in.
Signed and dated, l.l.
PROVENANCE
Private Collection, NY (current)
Jordan-Volpe Gallery, NY
Shearson Lehman Brothers, NY (as below, 1993)
Richard York Gallery, NY (on consignment, 1993)
Shearson Lehman Brothers, NY (1993)
Coe Kerr Gallery, NY (1992)
Berry-Hill Galleries, NY (1990)

[FIG. 47]

Moonrise on the New England Coast
Oil on canvas, 18 x 34½ in.
Signed and dated, l.l.
Photograph courtesy Richard York Gallery, NY

PROVENANCE

Mark Murray Fine Paintings, NY (1994)
Edward T. Wilson, Fund for Fine Arts,
MD (as below, 1993)
Richard York Gallery, NY (on consignment, 1993)
Edward T. Wilson, Fund for Fine
Arts, MD (1993)
William Doyle Galleries, NY (1989)
Joan Michelman Ltd., NY (1981)

[FIG. 48]

On the New Jersey Coast
Transparent and opaque watercolor
on paper, 15 x 25 in.
Signed and dated, l.l.
Photograph courtesy Vance Jordan Fine Art, Inc.

PROVENANCE

Vance Jordan Fine Art, Inc. (current)
Jordan-Volpe Gallery, NY (1990)
Butterfields, CA (1989)

On the North River
[PL. 30, page 96]
Oil on canvas, 20¼ x 36 in.
Signed and dated, l.l.; signed and
titled on verso

PROVENANCE

Private Collection, NY (current)
Richard York Gallery, NY (2000)

***A September Day on the Coast
(Point Judith, Rhode Island)***
[PL. 31, page 97]
Oil on canvas, 20 x 38 in.
Signed and dated, l.l.

PROVENANCE

Private Collection, MA (current)

Sunrise, Boston Harbor
Oil on canvas, 17¼ x 20 in.
Signed and dated, l.r.

PROVENANCE

Frank Schwarz & Son, PA (1988)
Biggs Museum of American Art, DE
Winterthur Museum, DE
Sewell C. Biggs, DE
Sotheby's, NY (1978)

LITERATURE

John A. H. Sweeney, "Paintings from
the Sewell C. Biggs Collection,"
The Magazine Antiques (April 1981),
pl. 18, p. 898.

[FIG. 49]

***Twilight along the River
(Twilight along the Coast)***
Oil on canvas, 24 x 20 in.
Signed and dated, l.r.
Photograph © Christie's Images, New York 2002

PROVENANCE

Christie's, NY (1998)
Wunderlich & Co., NY (1992)
Phillips, London (1992)
Private Collection, Isle of Wight,
Great Britain

LITERATURE

"Phillips London to Sell Painting by
American Francis Silva June 16,"
Antiques and The Arts Weekly (June 12,
1992), ill., p. 84.

Venetian Scene [circa 1879]

[FIG. 25, page 42]

Oil on canvas, 23 x 17 in.

Signed, l.r.

PROVENANCE

Richard Norton Gallery, IL (current)

Private Collection, CA (1985)

Venetian Scene

Oil on canvas, 50 x 42 in.

Signed and dated

PROVENANCE

Gallery Forty-Four, CT (1975)

[FIG. 50]

Wreck of a Whaler

Oil on canvas, 20 x 40 in.

Signed and dated, l.r.

Photograph courtesy Kennedy Galleries, NY

PROVENANCE

R. R. R. Associates, NH (1977)

Kennedy Galleries, NY (1972)

1880

**Along the Connecticut Shore
(On the Connecticut Shore)**

[PL. 32, page 98]

Transparent and opaque watercolor laid down on canvas, 18 x 28 in.

Signed and dated, l.l.

PROVENANCE

Mr. and Mrs. Carl F. Kalnow, OH (current)

Vallejo Gallery, CA

Christie's, NY (1996)

Catskill Mountains

Oil on canvas, 20 x 36 in.

Signed and dated, l.r.

PROVENANCE

Private Collection [unlocated]

LITERATURE

Donelson F. Hoopes, *The Beckoning Land, Nature and the American Artist: A Selection of Nineteenth Century Paintings*, exh. cat. (Atlanta: High Museum of Art, 1971), fig. 61, pp. 27, 85.

EXHIBITED

High Museum of Art, GA, "The Beckoning Land, Nature and the American Artist: A Selection of Nineteenth Century Paintings," 1971.

Fishing Boats at Moonlight

Oil on canvas, 14 x 12 in.

Signed and dated

PROVENANCE

Sotheby's, NY (1990)

Montgomery Gallery, CA

Low Tide

[PL. 33, page 99]

Oil on canvas, 19½ x 35½ in.

Signed and dated, l.r.

PROVENANCE

Bruce Museum of Arts and Science, CT, Bequest of George N. Morgan, 1946 (current)

George N. Morgan (1946)

Marsh Scene

[PL. 34, page 100]

Watercolor on paper, 10 x 20 in.

Signed and dated, l.r.

PROVENANCE

Maryann and Alvin Friedman, DC (current)

Berry-Hill Galleries, NY

Paul A. Kossey (1980)

Charles Lund, NJ

LITERATURE

Baur, 1980, fig. 22, p. 1031.

New York Harbor, New York

Oil on canvas, 12 x 20 in.

Signed and dated, l.r.

PROVENANCE

New-York Historical Society, NY (current)

Gallery Forty-Four, CT (1975)

LITERATURE

Richard J. Koke, compiler, *American Landscape and Genre Paintings in the New-York Historical Society: A Catalogue of the Collection, Including Historical, Narrative, and Marine Art* (New York: New-York Historical Society, 1982), vol. III, no. 2471, p. 139.

**An Old New England Seaport
(Boats to Let)**
Watercolor on paper, 17⅝ x 28⅛ in.
Signed and dated, l.l.
PROVENANCE
Quester Gallery, CT (1993)
EXHIBITED
American Watercolor Society Annual
Exhibition, NY, 1880, no. 346.

[FIG. 51]
An Old Town by the Sea
Oil on canvas, 24 x 44 in.
Signed and dated, l.r.
Photograph © Christie's Images, New York 2002
PROVENANCE
Christie's, NY (1993)
Sotheby's, NY (1987)
William Doyle Galleries, NY (1981)
Vose Galleries, MA
EXHIBITED
National Academy of Design Annual
Exhibition, NY, 1880, no. 601.

[FIG. 52]
On the Hudson
Oil on canvas, 20 x 36 in.
Signed and dated, l.l.
Photograph courtesy of Sotheby's, Inc. © 2002
PROVENANCE
Sotheby's (1984)

On the Hudson [circa 1880]
Oil on canvas, 16 x 23 in.
Signed, l.l.
PROVENANCE
Marine Arts Gallery, MA (1975)

Seabright from Galilee
Oil on canvas, 21 x 42 in.
Signed and dated, l.r.
PROVENANCE
Phillips, NY (2002)
R. H. Love Galleries, IL (2000)
H. V. Allison Galleries, NY (1989)
Christie's, NY (1979)
LITERATURE
Baur, 1980, fig. 18, p. 1028.

[FIG. 53]
Sunset off City Island [circa 1880]
Oil on canvas, 14 x 24¼ in.
Signed, l.r.
PROVENANCE
Santa Barbara Museum of Art, CA,
Museum Purchase, The Dicken
Fund in memory of Emily Rodgers
Davis (current)
Christie's, NY (1988)
Newhouse Galleries, NY
Frank Clancy, Jr. (1883)
Katherine Knox, CT
Charles A. Knox, CT

1881

**Evening (Twilight on the
New Jersey Shore)**
[FIG. 26, page 45]
Oil on canvas, 20¼ x 36 in.
Signed and dated, l.l.; signed and
titled on verso
Photograph courtesy of Sotheby's, Inc. © 2002
PROVENANCE
Sotheby's, NY (1981)
T. Edmund Garrity, MA (1980)
LITERATURE
Baur, 1980, fig. 19, p. 1029. [Dimensions
erroneously listed as 49 x 90 in.]

Long Branch, New Jersey (Ships off the Coast)
Watercolor on paper mounted on board, 8¾ x 11¾ in.
Signed and dated, l.l.
PROVENANCE
Christie's, NY (1985)
Butterfields, CA (1984)
Knoedler-Modarco, NY

A Midsummer's Twilight
Oil on canvas, 24¼ x 44 in.
Signed and dated, l.l.
PROVENANCE
Sotheby's, NY (1992)
Private Collection, PA (1935)
EXHIBITED
National Academy of Design Annual Exhibition, NY, 1881, no. 105.

Narragansett Bay
Oil on canvas, 21 x 39 in.
Signed and dated, l.r.
PROVENANCE
Harry Shaw Newman Gallery, NY (1948)
LITERATURE
Harry Shaw Newman Gallery, *Panorama* 4.1 (Aug.–Sept. 1948), no. 6.

1882

The Beach at Long Branch
Opaque watercolor, 10¾ x 20 in.
Signed and dated, l.l.
PROVENANCE
Sotheby's, NY (1995)

By the Seashore at Atlantic City
Mixed media, 6½ x 13¼ in.
Signed and dated, l.r.
PROVENANCE
Sotheby's, NY (1998)

Lakeside, Branchport, New York
Opaque watercolor on paper laid down on board, 6½ x 13½ in.
Signed, dated with title, l.l.
PROVENANCE
Christie's, NY (1995)

[FIG. 54]
Off Far Rockaway
Watercolor, 17 x 21¾ in.
Signed and dated, l.l.
Photograph ©Christie's Images, New York 2002
PROVENANCE
Christie's, NY (1995)

Seascape: Long Branch, Long Island
Watercolor, 10 x 19½ in.
Signed and dated with title, l.r.
PROVENANCE
Hirschl & Adler Galleries, NY (1989)

A Summer Day on the Coast (Afternoon along the Seashore)
[PL. 35, page 101]
Watercolor on paper, 10¼ x 19¾ in.
Signed and dated, l.l.
PROVENANCE
Vallejo Maritime Gallery, CA (current)
Frank H. Boos Gallery, MI (2001)
EXHIBITED
American Watercolor Society Annual Exhibition, NY, 1883, no. 436.

[FIG. 55]

The Beach at Seabright [circa 1883]
Transparent and opaque watercolor
on paper, 10½ x 20 in.
Signed with location, l.r.

PROVENANCE
Mr. and Mrs. Frederick Baekeland,
NY (1991)
Hirschl & Adler Galleries, NY (1978)
Sotheby's, NY (1978)

LITERATURE
Frederick Baekeland, *Images of America:
The Painter's Eye, 1833–1925*, exh. cat.
(Birmingham, Alabama: Birmingham
Museum of Art, 1991), no. 33, pp. 88–90.

EXHIBITED
Birmingham Museum of Art, AL,
"Images of America: The Painter's Eye,
1833–1925," 1991.

***Beers Cottage, Far Rockaway,
Long Island***
Oil on canvas, 25 x 44 in.
Signed and dated, l.l.

PROVENANCE
The Old Print Shop, NY (1955)

LITERATURE
The Old Print Shop, *Portfolio* 14.9
(May 1955), no. 29, p. 216.

Boats at Anchor
[PL. 36, page 102]
Oil on canvas, 16¾ x 14 in.
Signed and dated, l.r.

PROVENANCE
Elizabeth and Melville T. Hodder,
MA (current)

***By the Seaside, New Jersey Shore
(New Jersey Shore, Keyport, New Jersey)***
Oil on canvas, 26 x 40 in.
Signed and dated, l.l.

PROVENANCE
Deedee Wigmore Fine Art, Inc.,
NY (1992)

Cape Elizabeth, Maine
[PL. 37, page 103]
Oil on canvas, 7 x 15½ in.
Signed and dated, l.l.

PROVENANCE
Charles Butt, TX (current)

Clearing Off [circa 1883]
[PL. 38, page 104]
Oil on canvas, 20⅜ x 38 in.
Signed, l.r.

PROVENANCE
Berry-Hill Galleries, NY (current)
Mr. and Mrs. Frederick Baekeland, NY (1991)

LITERATURE
Frederick Baekeland, *Images of America:
The Painter's Eye, 1833–1925*, exh. cat.
(Birmingham, Alabama: Birmingham
Museum of Art, 1991), no. 32, pp. 88–90.

EXHIBITED
Birmingham Museum of Art, AL,
"Images of America: The Painter's Eye,
1833–1925," 1991.

Holding Her Course
Oil on canvas, 16 x 12 in.
Signed and dated, l.l.

PROVENANCE
Christie's, NY (1997)
D. B. Butler and Co., Inc., NY

***Off Rockaway Beach (Off Far
Rockaway)***
[PL. 39, page 105]
Oil on canvas, 14 x 26 in.
Signed and dated, l.l.

PROVENANCE
Melinda and Howard Godel, NY (current)
Howard Antiques, NY (1985)
Marshall Henis

EXHIBITED
Godel & Co., NY, "Nineteenth-Century
Landscapes and Luminist Views," 1992.

***Off the Coast (Sunset on a Rocky
Coast; Coastline at Sunset)***
[PL. 40, page 106]
Oil on canvas, 20 x 36 in.
Signed and dated, l.l.

PROVENANCE
Private Collection, MD (current)
Richard York Gallery, NY (1992)
Private Collection, PA
Grand Central Art Galleries, Inc.,
NY (1983)
Sotheby's, NY (1978)

Old and Abandoned
Oil on canvas, 17¼ x 26½ in.
Signed and dated, l.r.

PROVENANCE
Christie's, NY (1988)

[FIG. 56]

Point Judith, Rhode Island
Watercolor, 10¾ x 20 in.
Signed and dated, l.r.
Photograph courtesy of Sotheby's, Inc. ©2002
PROVENANCE
Sotheby's, NY (1997)
EXHIBITED
American Watercolor Society Annual
Exhibition, NY, 1884, no. 636.

Seabright, New Jersey
Watercolor on board, 8 x 14¾ in.
Signed and dated with title, l.l.
PROVENANCE
Hirschl & Adler, NY
Christie's, NY (1979)
LITERATURE
Baur, 1980, fig. 20, p. 1030.

Shore Scene
[PL. 41, page 107]
Oil on canvas, 17 x 26 in.
Signed and dated, l.l.
PROVENANCE
Private Collection, AR (current)
Berry-Hill Galleries, NY (1996)

1884

Seascape
Oil, 20 x 36 in.
PROVENANCE
Mrs. Elisha Gee, TN (1985)

1885

[FIG. 57]

**A Summer Afternoon at Long Branch
(A Summer Afternoon at Long Beach;
A Sunny Summer's Day, Long Branch,
New Jersey)**
Oil on canvas, 24 x 44 in.
Signed and dated, l.l.
PROVENANCE
Mr. and Mrs. Wilbur L. Ross, Jr.,
NY (1980)
Sporting Gallery, Inc., VA (1975)
LITERATURE
John I. H. Baur, *A Mirror of Creation:
150 Years of American Nature Painting*,
exh. cat. (New York: Friends of
American Art in Religion, Inc., 1980),
no. 18.
Baur, 1980, pl. 2, p. 1019
John Wilmerding, *American Light:
The Luminist Movement, 1850–1875*
(New York: Harper & Row;

Washington, DC: National Gallery of
Art, 1980), fig. 50, pp. 49–50.
EXHIBITED
Vatican Museums, Vatican City State,
"A Mirror of Creation: 150 Years of
American Nature Painting," 1980.

1886

**Autumn Afternoon on the New
England Coast**
[FIG. 34, page 58]
Oil on canvas, 42 x 58 in.
Signed and dated, l.r.
Photograph ©Christie's Images, New York 2002
PROVENANCE
Guarisco Gallery, DC (1994)
Christie's, NY (1992)
Mrs. George Arden (1980)
Sotheby's, NY (1976)

2. Undated Paintings

[FIG. 58]
Afternoon Sun
Oil on canvas, 12 x 24 in.
Signed, l.l.
Photograph courtesy Vose Galleries, MA

PROVENANCE
Vose Galleries, MA

Along the Coast
Oil on canvas, 12 x 22 in.
Signed, l.l.
PROVENANCE
Christie's, NY (1981)

Along the Shore (Passing Shower)
[FIG. 33, page 57]
Oil on canvas, 20⅛ x 36⅛ in.
Signed, l.r.
Photograph © Christie's Images, New York 2002

PROVENANCE
Christie's, NY (1993)
Christie's, NY (1984)
Sotheby's, NY (1981)
Vose Galleries, MA

At Nantasket, Massachusetts, Misty Morning
Oil on paper, 6½ x 9½ in.
Signed, l.r.
PROVENANCE
Sotheby's, NY (1996)
Mabell G. Clarke Smith
Edward A. M. Clarke, NY

At Sunset
Oil, 16 x 20 in.
Signed
PROVENANCE
Sotheby's, NY (1996)

Beach Scene, Cohasset, Massachusetts
Oil, 8 x 12 in.
PROVENANCE
Elton Yasuna, MA (1975)

Boats on the Hudson (The Hudson River near Piermont, New York)
Oil on canvas, 9⅛ x 17¹⁵/₁₆ in.
Signed, l.l.
PROVENANCE
Brooklyn Museum of Art, NY, on extended loan to the New York Governor's Mansion (current)
Bernard Danenberg Galleries, NY (1971)

LITERATURE
Brooklyn Museum, *The Brooklyn Museum, American Paintings: A Complete Illustrated Listing of Works in the Museum's Collection* (Brooklyn: Brooklyn Museum of Art, 1979), p. 104.
Anon., "Recent Accessions of American and Canadian Museums, Oct.–Dec. 1970," *Art Quarterly* 34.2 (1971), p. 251, ill. p. 264.

Boston Light (Lighthouse and Rowboats)
Oil on canvas, 19 x 26 in.
Signed, l.l.
PROVENANCE
Marine Arts Gallery, MA (1971)

[FIG. 59]

Coast near Cape Ann
Oil on canvas, 9 x 18 in.
Signed, l.r.
Photograph © Christie's Images, New York 2002
PROVENANCE
William Doyle Galleries, NY (1989)
Christie's, NY (1986)

[FIG. 60]

**Coastal View at Sunset (Cape Ann
View at Sunset)**
Oil on canvas, 9 x 18 in.
Signed
PROVENANCE
Private Collection, IL (current)
Mark L. Brock, MA (2001)
Debra Force Fine Art, Inc., NY
(as agent, 2001)
Skinner, MA (2000)

**A Coastal View with Sailboats
(Coastal Scene; Seascape)**
Oil on canvas, 14 x 24 in.
Signed, l.l.
PROVENANCE
Christie's, NY (1989)
Coe Kerr Gallery, NY (1977)
Knoedler-Modarco, NY

Crashing Surf
Watercolor on paper, 11¼ x 26½ in.
Signed, l.r.
PROVENANCE
Spanierman Gallery, NY (current)

[FIG. 61]

Dusk on the Hudson
Watercolor on paper, 8⅛ x 12⅜ in.
Photograph courtesy of Sotheby's, Inc. ©2002
PROVENANCE
Sotheby's, NY (1997)
Christie's, NY (1985)

Early Morning on the River
Oil, 8 x 12 in.
PROVENANCE
Baker-Pisano Collection, NY (1976)

Far Rockaway Beach
Oil on canvas, 14½ x 24 in.
Signed, l.r.
PROVENANCE
Sotheby's, NY (1990)
Richard A. Bourne Co., Inc., MA (1977)
Lee B. Anderson, NY (1967)

Far Rockaway Inlet
Watercolor, 7 x 9½ in.
Signed
PROVENANCE
Louisiana Auction Exchange, Inc.,
LA (1996)
Christie's, NY (1996)

Fishing Shacks: Sunset
Oil, 14 x 24 in.
Signed, l.l.
PROVENANCE
Hirschl & Adler Galleries, NY (1978)

[FIG. 62]

Gloucester Dawn
Oil, 9 x 18 in.
Signed
Photograph © Christie's Images, New York 2002
PROVENANCE
Christie's, NY (1993)

[FIG. 63]

Haverstraw Bay
Oil on canvas, 12 x 24 in.
Signed, l.r.
PROVENANCE
Mark Murray Fine Paintings, NY and
Edward T. Wilson, Fund for Fine Arts,
MD (1996)
Sotheby's, NY (1995)
Kennedy Galleries, NY (1978)

Heading Out
Oil on canvas, 12 x 10 in.
Signed, l.r.
PROVENANCE
Richard A. Bourne Co., Inc., MA (1979)

Hudson River at Kingston Point
[PL. 42, page 108]
Oil on canvas, 14 x 24 in.
Signed, l.r.
PROVENANCE
Mr. and Mrs. David MacCallum,
NY (current)
Christie's, NY (1992)

Hudson River Landscape
Oil, dimensions unknown
PROVENANCE
Private Collection [unlocated]

Lakeside Cottage
Opaque watercolor, 7 x 13 in.
Signed
PROVENANCE
Christie's, NY (1995)

Landscape
Medium and dimensions unknown
PROVENANCE
Roberson's, NY (1996)

Late Afternoon
[FIG. 30, page 52]
Oil on canvas, 18 x 30 in.
Signed, l.r.
Photograph courtesy of Sotheby's, Inc. ©2002
PROVENANCE
Sotheby's, NY (1983)

Lower New York Harbor
Oil on canvas, 12 x 10 in.
Signed, l.l.
PROVENANCE
Questroyal Fine Art, NY

[FIG. 64]

Misty Morning in New York Bay
Oil on board, 6¼ x 12¼ in.
Signed, l.r.; signed and titled on verso
Photograph ©Christie's Images, New York 2002
PROVENANCE
Christie's, NY (1993)
Christie's, NY (1990)

Moonlight, Cape Ann
Oil on canvas, 12¼ x 24¼ in.
Signed, l.l.
PROVENANCE
Sotheby's, NY (1986)
Marine Arts Gallery, MA

[FIG. 65]

Moonlight, New York Harbor
Oil on canvas, 14 x 23½ in.
Signed, l.r.
PROVENANCE
Private Collection [unlocated]
David Findlay, Jr., Inc., NY
LITERATURE
Baur, 1980, fig. 11, p. 1025.

Moonrise (Moonrise, Cape Ann)
[FIG. 14, page 30]
Oil on canvas, 12 x 24 in.
Signed, l.l.
Photograph courtesy Kennedy Galleries, NY
PROVENANCE
Vose Galleries, MA
Kennedy Galleries, NY (1970)

The Narrows at Staten Island
Oil on canvas, 12 x 24 in.
Signed, l.r.
PROVENANCE
Parnassus Gallery, NY (1955)

[FIG. 66]

Off Eastern Point Light
Oil on canvas, 18 x 30 in.
Photograph courtesy Vose Galleries, MA
PROVENANCE
Vose Galleries, MA (1981)
Nathaniel Harris, MA (1981)

Old Wreck at Long Branch
Oil on board, 5 x 11 in.
Signed, l.r.; titled on verso
PROVENANCE
Sotheby's, NY (1986)

On the Coast
Oil on board, 4½ x 8¾ in.
Signed, l.r.
PROVENANCE
Sotheby's, NY (1996)
Mabell G. Clarke Smith
Edward A. M. Clarke, NY

On the Hudson River, Nyack
[PL. 43, page 109]
Oil on canvas, 20 x 36 in.
Signed, l.l.
PROVENANCE
Private Collection, MA (current)

Palisades of the Hudson River
[PL. 44, page 110]
Oil on canvas, 9 x 18½ in.
Signed, l.r.
PROVENANCE
Private Collection (current)
Berry-Hill Galleries, NY (1993)
North Point Gallery, CA (1992)

Pilot Returning to Shore
Medium unknown, 24¼ x 40¼ in.
PROVENANCE
Samuel Lowe Antiques, MA (1973)

**Robin's Reef Lighthouse off
Tomkinsville, New York Harbor**
[PL. 45, page 111]
Oil on canvas, 9 x 18 in.
Signed, l.r.
PROVENANCE
Berry-Hill Galleries, NY (current)
Kennedy Galleries, NY

Rockaway Beach
Medium and dimensions unknown
Signed, l.l.
PROVENANCE
Paul Magriel (1957)
LITERATURE
John I. H. Baur, "From Apples to
Goddesses: The Paul Magriel
Collection," *Art in America* 45.4
(Winter 1957/58), p. 21.

Rocky Cliffs and Shore at Sunset
Oil on board, 4¾ x 9 in.
Signed, l.r.
PROVENANCE
Northeast Auctions, NH (2001)

Sailing at Sunset
Oil, 20 x 16 in.
Signed
PROVENANCE
Shannon's Fine Art Auctioneers,
CT (2001)

Sailing into the Sunset
Oil on canvas, 21¼ x 32 in.
Signed, l.l.
PROVENANCE
Raydon Gallery, NY (1982)
Sotheby's, NY (1981)
Edward Lamb, OH

Sailing Vessels off Cape Ann
Oil on canvas, 13½ x 23½ in.
Signed, l.l.
PROVENANCE
George Arden, NY (1980)

Schooner on a River
[PL. 46, page 112]
Oil on board, 7 x 5 in.
Signed, l.r.
PROVENANCE
Edwin and Sarah Pomphrey, NJ (current)

Seascape
Opaque and transparent watercolor
on paper laid on canvas, 15 x 25 in.
Signed and dated [unknown date; erro-
neously listed as 1890 in advertisement]
PROVENANCE
Henry B. Holt, NJ (1980)

Seascape
Oil, 11 x 16 in.
PROVENANCE
Mystic Fine Arts, CT (1997)

Seascape (Coney Island Beach)
Oil on canvas, 20¼ x 36⅛ in.
Signed, l.l.
PROVENANCE
Sheldon Memorial Art Gallery and
Sculpture Garden, University of
Nebraska-Lincoln, NE (current)
Carl and Jane Rohman (2000)
Sotheby's, NY (1981)
Alexander Gallery, NY (1981)

Seascape at Sunset
Oil, 10 x 12 in.
Signed
PROVENANCE
Sotheby's, NY (1998)

[FIG. 67]

**Seascape—Baker's Island near New
Bedford (Sunset, Baker's Island,
Salem, Massachusetts; Lighthouse in
View of Baker's Island, New Bedford)**
Oil on canvas, 20 x 38 in.
Signed, l.r.
Photograph courtesy Kennedy Galleries, NY
PROVENANCE
Steven Straw Co., NH (1971)
Marine Arts Gallery, MA (1971)
Kennedy Galleries, NY (1970)

Seascape: Long Branch, New Jersey
Watercolor, 10 x 19¼ in.
Signed, l.r.
PROVENANCE
Hirschl & Adler Galleries, NY (1978)

**Seascape, White Island Light, Isles
of Shoals**
Oil on canvas, 21 x 28 in.
Signed, l.l.
PROVENANCE
Private Collection, DC (current)
Vose Galleries, MA
Michael Kent, PA

[FIG. 68]

**Seascape with Lighthouse, Sailboats
and Rowboats**
Oil on canvas, 19 x 26 in.
Signed, l.l.
Photograph courtesy Kennedy Galleries, NY
PROVENANCE
Kennedy Galleries, NY (1970)

Seascape with Sailboats
Oil on canvas, 14 x 12 in.
Signed
PROVENANCE
D. B. Butler and Co., Inc., NY

Seascape with Sailboats
[PL. 47, page 113]
Oil on panel, 4⅝ x 7⅞ in.
Signed, l.l.
PROVENANCE
Robert C. Lyster, NY (current)
D. B. Butler and Co., Inc., NY

[FIG. 69]

**Shipwreck on a Sandy Beach
(Past Her Glory)**
Oil on canvas, 18¼ x 36¼ in.
Signed, l.r.
Photograph courtesy of Sotheby's, Inc. ©2002

PROVENANCE
Private Collection, NJ (current)
Sotheby's, NY (1998)
Masco Corporation, IL (1998)
Alexander Gallery, NY (1994)
Butterfields, CA (1993)

Shoreline, Early Evening
[FIG. 28, page 48]
Oil on canvas, 18½ x 34½ in.
Signed, l.l.
Photograph ©Christie's Images, New York 2002

PROVENANCE
Private Collection, CT (current)
Christie's, NY (1983)

Shoreline Scene
Oil on canvas, 20 x 36 in.

PROVENANCE
Private Collection [unlocated]

Shore Scene
Oil on canvas, 16 x 27½ in.
Signed, l.l.

PROVENANCE
Private Collection [unlocated]

Southern New Jersey Coast
Watercolor, 10¾ x 28½ in.
Signed

PROVENANCE
William Doyle Galleries, NY (2000)
Christie's, NY (1992)

[FIG. 70]

**A Summer Squall (Ships Approaching
Atlantic City)**
Oil, 20¼ x 36 in.
Signed, l.r.
Photograph ©Christie's Images, New York 2002

PROVENANCE
Christie's, NY (1994)
Sotheby's, NY (1984)

**Sundown, Summer Seascape,
Cape Ann**
Oil on canvas, 20½ x 40 in.
Signed, l.l.

PROVENANCE
Kennedy Galleries, NY

Sunset
Oil, 20 x 36 in.
Signed

PROVENANCE
Sotheby's, NY (1990)

**Sunset on a Mountain Lake
(Lake Landscape)**
Oil on canvas, 5 x 10 in.
Signed, l.l.

PROVENANCE
Sotheby's, NY (1979)
Sotheby's, NY (1948)

Twilight
Oil, 22 x 18 in.
Signed, l.r.

PROVENANCE
Private Collection [unlocated]

Venice Scene
Oil on canvas, 23 x 17 in.
Signed, l.r.

PROVENANCE
Richard Norton Gallery, IL (current)
Helen M. Broan, CA (1985)

A View of Storm King on the Hudson
Oil on canvas, dimensions unknown

PROVENANCE
Private Collection [unlocated]

Waiting for the Rest of the Party
Oil on board, 4½ x 8 in.
Signed, l.r.

PROVENANCE
Sotheby's, NY (1996)
Mabell G. Clarke Smith
Edward A. M. Clarke, NY

Women Walking along the Shore
[FIG. 15, page 31]
Oil on canvas, 12 x 24 in.
Signed, l.l.
Photograph courtesy Kennedy Galleries, NY

PROVENANCE
Kennedy Galleries, NY (1969)

3. Peabody Essex Museum Collection

Through several gifts to the then separate Peabody Museum and Essex Institute, Marie Antoinette (Nettie) Silva created what is today by far the largest single collection of preparatory works by Francis A. Silva, her father. Her reasons for splitting the donation between the two museums remain a mystery, but the consolidation of the two institutions in 1992 has at last reunited Nettie Silva's collection. In addition to the many preparatory works given by the artist's daughter, the museum has also received a major oil entitled *Two Unidentified Coasting Vessels* (c. 1870, acc. no. M8943, Pl. 4), listed in the inventory above. The oil was a gift of Charles Henry Cooper in 1956 and rounds out the museum's collection.

As part of the research for this exhibition, a database was compiled surveying the museum's several hundred pencil, watercolor, and oil sketches. The collection is divided under four accession numbers corresponding to the separate gifts. One of the numbers, M8943, refers to the *Two Unidentified Coasting Vessels* alone. The following description offers a brief summary of the materials in the other three:

Acc. No. 123351, gift of Miss Marie Antoinette Silva, 1938
A: Sketchbook, 5⅝ x 9 in., 79 pages, all dated sketches are 1871
B: 13 loose oil sketches, various sizes, only 2 are dated, both 1870
C: 20 loose watercolor sketches, various sizes, dates range from 1873 to 1882
D: 35 loose sketches in different media, various sizes, dates from 1869 to 1885

Acc. No. 125248, gift of Miss Marie Antoinette Silva, 1942
54 loose sketches, various media and sizes, dates from 1867 to 1883

Acc. No. M8871, gift of Miss Marie Antoinette Silva, 1942, 1951, and 1952
1: Sketchbook, 4 x 7 in., 89 pages, dated works from 1871 to 1884
2: Sketchbook, 5½ x 9 in., 81 pages, dated works from 1871 to 1883
3: Sketchbook, 4 x 6¼ in., 59 pages, dated works from 1874 to 1885
4: Sketchbook, 4½ x 7 in., 84 pages, dated works from 1878 to 1883
5: Sketchbook, 3½ x 5½ in., 40 pages, dated works from 1878 to 1882
6: Sketchbook, 5½ x 8¾ in., 168 pages, dated works from 1879 to 1885
F1-6: 6 folders of loose sketches, 48 sketches total, various media and sizes, dates from 1868 to 1884

[N.B. Sketchbook "pages" refer to sides, not leaves. Each leaf is two pages. Also, several books have additional pages of different dimensions and different kinds of paper tipped in.]

[FIG. 71]
Causeway (verso), n.d.
(Acc. No. 125248.14)

Published on the occasion
of the exhibition

Francis A. Silva (1835–1886),
In His Own Light

at BERRY-HILL GALLERIES, INC.
11 East 70th Street
New York, New York 10021
Telephone 212.744.2300
Fax 212.744.2838
www.berry-hill.com

April 24 – June 28, 2002

Copyright © Berry-Hill Galleries, Inc., 2002
Library of Congress Control Number:
2002102016

DESIGN
Anthony McCall Associates

PRINTING
Toppan Printing Company America, Inc.

PHOTOGRAPHY
Helga Photo Studio, New Jersey
Eduardo Calderon Photography, Seattle

FRONTISPIECE
Schooner Passing Castle Island, Boston Harbor,
1874 (detail)

FRONT AND BACK COVERS
On the Hudson River, Nyack, n.d. (detail)